WINDOWS ONTO ...

September 28th
1987.

For John

With Gratitude
al Affection

Robert Canterbury

Robert Runcie

WINDOWS ONTO GOD

Compiled and arranged by
Eileen Mable

First published 1983
SPCK
Holy Trinity Church
Marylebone Road
London NW1 4DU

British Library Cataloguing in Publication Data

Runcie, Robert
  Windows onto God
  1. Christian life
  I. Title
  248.4   BV4501.2

  ISBN 0-281-04076-1

Printed in Great Britain by
Photobooks (Bristol) Ltd
Barton Manor, St Philips, Bristol

Contents

🔲🔲🔲🔲

Archbishop's Foreword

A NEWLY APPOINTED archbishop emerges from relative obscurity into the glare of media scrutiny. Very soon, he is expected to pronounce on a bewildering range of subjects from factory farming to the dental problems of Eskimos.

This is obviously a task beyond the competence of one man. A modern archbishop, therefore, has to be a good listener and he has to be quick to identify those who have more ample experience of particular problems and advice to offer. This is especially important since archbishops still have opportunities to touch a constituency much wider than that of regular churchgoers. He must use his platform on behalf of the whole Church and struggle to avoid becoming a platitude machine by maintaining a conversation with people who have more time for reflection on the problems of the day.

The following speeches and addresses illustrate my debt to many people. Much has happened during these past three years: royal occasions, war, the papal visit, as well as the familiar and enjoyable round of parish visits and confirmations in my own diocese of Canterbury. Some of the pieces in this book were prepared in haste under great pressure and it has not been possible to devote very much time to revising them. I am therefore more than usually grateful to the editorial wisdom of Eileen Mable, who has encouraged me to think that some of this material may be worth preserving and without whom this collection would never have seen the light of day.

As always, however, my most important debt is to those who make effective work possible by the support of their affection and their prayers. I depend more and more on this invisible but palpable encouragement.

Robert Cantuar
April 1983

Christian Authority

'AND THE ANGEL said to Mary, "Jesus shall be great and shall be called the Son of the Highest, and the Lord God shall give him the throne of his father David."' Jesus was given a throne. That means he was given authority, but authority of what kind, and how did he come by it? On the day of his own enthronement,[1] an archbishop does well to ponder such matters, which touch not only him but the whole Christian community. The Church exists as an embodiment of Jesus Christ. It exists to express God's love for men and to draw men to an even deeper love of God. We are doing this work as we become more like Jesus Christ. Our proper authority comes by being like him and our way to a throne must be like his way.

Of course the Church has often tried to take short cuts to authority, enforcing respect and obedience by worldly means and so obscuring the face of God. I have inherited a substantial supply of weapons which once equipped the archbishop's private army. Men of power sat in that chair and their pikes now decorate the walls of Lambeth Palace. Museum pieces? But the temptation to gain the Church's end by using the world's means is still with us. We are tempted to organize ourselves like any other party or pressure group, to establish sharper dividing lines between those who are members and those who are not, to compete more aggressively for attention from the public, to recruit new members with a strident self-confidence which suggests that we have nothing to learn, to persuade with a loud voice rather than with the quiet reason of the heart. Salesmanship may seem a sensible strategy for securing the Church's prosperity and survival as an institution. I do not wish to be misunderstood. Any Church which does not make demands on those who call themselves Christian,

---

[1] Sermon preached at the enthronement, Canterbury Cathedral, 25 March 1980

and which does not desire to draw others into the company of those who know God and love him, is deaf to the resounding commission of the Lord which has just been read [Matthew 28.16–20].

We have spiritual treasure in the words of life; but it matters desperately how our treasure is shared, how those ends are pursued and how the Church seeks to exercise authority. Aggression and compulsion was not the way of Jesus Christ, the homeless wanderer, the Son of God who came among us in the form of a servant and shared our suffering. When you are a friend to everyone, whether they belong to your group or not, when you have felt suffering, poverty and sickness, not necessarily in your own person but by being a friend to those who suffer, then you are led into a depth of love which the hard-boiled never glimpse or attain. This deep unsentimental love – part toughness, part sensitivity – has in itself an authority which makes people question and change the way in which they are living. You can see it in the life of our contemporary, Mother Teresa of Calcutta. She is almost powerless, but she speaks and acts with Christ's own authority. She is hugely influential in a world distracted and confused by the strident clamour of pressure groups and rival theories.

If the Church acts as if it possessed its answers to life's problems tied up in neat packages, it may be heard for a time. It may rally some waverers; but its influence will not last. It will confirm others in their suspicion and hostility. To them it will mean that the Church, like every other human institution, is making a bid for power. Even when we speak, as we must, the life-giving truths in the precious words of Scripture handed down to us, those words can lack authority because what we are will deny what we say – and we shall not ourselves be able to understand deeply what we are saying. For the Church to have the authority of Jesus Christ, it must not merely repeat the definition of belief distilled by our forerunners – vitally important though this is. The Church must live now as Jesus Christ would live now.

Like Isaiah of old, we must begin by admitting that we have fallen short of the vision which is given to us; but his response was, 'Woe is me, for I am a man of unclean lips and I dwell in the midst of a people of unclean lips'. This penitence should be a constant note of our life in the Church. Today we celebrate the response to God's call made by a young woman of no great family or education. She was able to hear God speaking in a way which was not, and is not, possible for the worldly-wise with the crust of success which cakes the eyes and covers the ears. 'How shall these things be?' Wonder, longing, obedience are the mixture in Mary, the first to respond to the call of God in Christ. So the strange authority of Christ's Church begins not in the assumption that we possess all the answers but in our recognition of our poverty of spirit. From that can come a real longing to hear God speak. One of the major themes of the New Testament is that a sense of possession gets in the way of spiritual growth. Our lives must be full of longing as we struggle to become more Christ-like.

One task which is going to occupy much of my time is gaining some knowledge of the worldwide Anglican Communion. There are nearly seventy million Anglicans spread in every continent with a great variety of styles of life. I am soon to attend an enthronement in Central Africa of an archbishop for a new French-speaking province of the Anglican Communion. Archbishop Bezaleri will be enthroned in very different circumstances. No cathedral, let alone trumpets, there. This service in Canterbury, so carefully prepared, so magnificently beautiful, speaks eloquently of the glory of God and the dignity which God gives to men by loving them. Its pageantry speaks, too, of English tradition of which we are rightly proud – countries, like individuals, only thrive if they are loved, and I am proud of a religious tradition which, in attempting to blend freedom and religious conviction, has coloured a nation's life and sometimes been paid for in blood. But it may be that the simple service to which I shall go in Africa will prove more eloquent about the uncluttered way in which the Church should live now, about the unpretentious character of real Christian authority. There is no place in our understanding of authority for the Archbishop of Canterbury to visit Africa like some reigning monarch descending on a viceroy. I shall be there to share what we have in

England with our brothers and sisters and to learn what they have to teach us about personal discipline and sacrifice, and about the fresh joy of being a new follower of Christ.

The same approach will be vital in relationship with other Christian Churches. It fills my heart with great hope to see so many Christian leaders assembled here from every part of the globe. And it would be insensitive if I did not share the shock at the murder of Archbishop Romero: a sober reminder that life and death for the gospel are still the way Christians are called to change the world.

The vitality and spiritual energy represented here could be a great force for world peace and social justice. Much is being done already, but we are hampered by our divisions, and the worldwide Christian Church will not be able to speak the authority of Christ until it speaks with one voice. Few would dissent from that, but how is it to be achieved? I believe that negotiations aimed at merging institutions have only a limited usefulness without the sort of work in which I have had a tiny share in recent years as, across ancient theological misunderstandings and sharp political frontiers, we have tried to discern the mind of Christ. Brotherhood grows not by two people obsessively discussing each other's personality but by two people looking in the same direction, working together and experiencing new things together. A humble willingness to work in this way and to accept disappointment when progress seems slow has been a mark of the ministry of both my predecessors, Archbishop Ramsey and Archbishop Coggan. They both saw that true Christian unity came from the sheep rallying to the call of the Master and not from the sheep deciding to huddle together against the storm.

Christ does not only draw us closer to our fellow Christians. If we are to be followers of him, we shall be led into friendship with the host of thoughtful and honest men and women outside the Church who are aware that the world is out of joint, perilously close to famine and war, that the streets are more and more dangerous for the weak, that families are breaking up, perhaps that their own lives are in a mess. Christ draws us close to many people who seek God and who may be doing his will more effectively than those who can say to Christ, 'Lord, Lord'.

You know how sometimes in an English garden you find a maze. The trouble is to get to the centre of all those hedges. It is easy to get lost. I had a dream of a maze. There were some people very close to the centre; only a single hedge separated them from the very heart of the maze but they could not find a way through. They had taken a wrong turn right at the very beginning and would have to return to the gate if they were to make any further progress. But just outside the gate others were standing. They were further away from the heart of the maze, but they would be there sooner than the party that fretted and fumed inside. I long to be able to speak, while archbishop, with men and women who stand outside the Christian Church. I would say to them, 'You can teach us much if together we could look for the secret of the maze-like muddle in which the world finds itself'. I ask for your prayers that I may be given the grace to speak like that and to listen.

But I must stand also not at the edge but at the very centre of the Christian company as supporter and encourager – and my particular heroes among those who speak for Christ and follow his way are found in places where priest and people, men and women, of different ages, change the atmosphere of their local community, drawing people to Christ by the authority that their honesty and love and service win for them. This way of living and sharing, admitting our own failings and our longings, is not what people expect from those who sit on thrones. 'Speak out, condemn, denounce', is what is expected. But the throne of Jesus is a mercy-seat. It stands firm against all the vileness of the world but it stands also for compassion. The way of Jesus means reverencing people whether they belong to our party or not. The strategy of Jesus means changing lives with love.

This is a hard way and people tend to want it only in theory. The cry is, 'The Church must give a firm lead'. Yes. it must – a firm lead against rigid thinking, a judging temper of mind, the disposition to oversimplify the difficult and complex problems. If the Church gives Jesus Christ's sort of lead, it will not be popular. It may even be despised for failing to grasp the power which is offered to it in the confusions and fears of our contemporaries. But it will be a Church not only close to the mind of Jesus, it will find itself constantly pushing back the frontiers of the possible. 'For with God nothing is impossible.' And it will be a Church confident with the promise of Jesus, 'Lo, I am with you always, even to the end of the ages'. That is why this is a service of glorious celebration.

But the personal dedication around which it revolves is a dedication to the way of Jesus Christ, and the support of all who share with me in this day will find no better expression than in the personal dedication of all who can follow with me in that way. It is not just the pontifex – that rather grand title which simply means 'Bridge-builder'. We are all to be the bridge-builders of the world: the bridge between God and man, found for us in the face of Jesus Christ; the bridge between the Jesus of history and the living Christ of our experience; the bridge between Christian and Christian; the bridge between Christians and a world where our allies will be the God-seekers, the peacemakers, and friends of the poor. But if you would seek to put the world to rights, do you begin with some other person or with yourself? It is a day to remember that the confrontation of God with man calls out not the interest of the spectator but the fresh and renewed response of the seeker. 'Here am I, send me. I am the Lord's servant. As you have spoken – so be it.'

THE CHURCH

Synodical Government

◙◙◙◙

WITH THIS GROUP of sessions[1] we come to the end of a
General Synod and the completion of a decade of synodical
government. It is a time for reflection. When William
Temple and Dick Sheppard founded the Life and Liberty
movement neither had much patience with legal structures,
ecclesiastical bureaucracy or parliamentary-style assemblies. Dick Sheppard remained amazed that he, of all
people, should have wanted an Act of Parliament and a
church legislative body. He wanted them only as a way to
set God's people free from the complexity of the past so
that they might know a Christian liberty and a new spiritual
energy might be released. William Temple recalled that
they had a vision of a Church where there would be a
sharing of material resources, freedom to develop new
ways of worship, a new search for Christian unity and a
renewed mission to the nation.

Today it is all too easy to be critical of synodical
government and to forget just how far it has allowed the
Church of England to reshape its life. There has been, for
example, one quiet revolution in our affairs. So quiet that
some may not have noticed it happening. It has been the
gradual elimination of that element of condescension in
our church life which some of our critics noted and which
they found so unlovely and even unchristian, and the
emergence of new partnerships. The ARCIC Statement on
Authority has it: 'The perception of God's will for his
Church does not belong only to the ordained ministry but
is shared by all its members.' This can remain in the realm
of rhetoric. We seek to give it value by a new sense of
sharing which has been apparent in the past ten years.
Within the lifetime of this Synod, the Church has achieved
substantial liberty to choose its bishops, create a new

[1] From the presidential address to General Synod, July 1980

liturgy and reshape its financial and pastoral administration. These things have been done, moreover, without forfeiting the old responsibilities which we have in the public life of the nation. All these are real achievements.

This Synod has, of course, not lacked courage in the range of its debate of international and social issues. I hope we shall never be tempted to withdraw from that scene. The Methodist Conference has recently set us a good example in that respect. The value of such outward-looking debate may be symbolic, educational and morale-supporting for individuals and groups who are closely involved and who are better informed about the issues than we are. However, some of the most critical problems for the nature of our nation and the world are difficult to handle, boring to present and do not yield short-cut solutions. We are easily scared off them. And the cry is heard: it is too complicated; it is too political; we do not know all the facts; we shall be at the mercy of the emotional appeal. Yet Christians are called to kindle consciences in a longterm way if we are to be true to our brethren in the past and in other places who have been pioneers of a more Christian society. There will be divisions of opinion among us, but I could wish that we might set an example, not of smothering but of handling conflict. Perhaps the Synod is still too much structured on the assumption that, on this and other matters, the best we can hope for is a majority victory when the division bell rings. Does not the cry 'divide' make us set our sights too low?

Here is another problem of which we must constantly be aware. However much the social influence of the Church has declined in society, we remain a powerful and wealthy institution which nevertheless has to fulfil a fundamental commitment of the gospel to speak for the vulnerable, the inarticulate and those who are weak in bargaining power – a bias to those who are, or feel, excluded or put down. I hope that we shall not feel that our wider awareness calls for frequent pronouncements as a Synod on contemporary life and manners. Quite apart from the fact that the world discounts overmuch exhortation from the Churches, it is also quick to detect that censoriousness is not an authentic note of the gospel. It is simply a matter of Christian

integrity that we should be slow to pass judgement, ready
to think out each matter carefully and theologically, and be
prepared to see how a principle stands in our own church
life – that means what we are doing about it – before we
undertake to teach others.

So much for my commitment to, and views about,
synodical government, but I hope that you will allow me a
word on that subject which has occupied the greater part of
our time in recent years but on which I must be one of the
few bishops who have not made any contribution during
the past decade. I would not want you to be ignorant of
where I stand. I do not regret *all* the recent public reactions
to the work of this Synod on liturgical reform. They are a
reminder that the worship of God not only expresses the
life of the Church but can nourish the soul of a people. The
power of sacred association penetrates into deep affections
of the heart and stirrings of the conscience, and those who
cling to what they know do so from no unworthy motives.
Nor can someone who has travelled, as I have done, in
countries hostile to the Christian religion, be unaware of
the power of an ancient liturgy to carry faith and hope
from age to age. But their situation is not ours, and I do
regret some of the unfair imputations that pass to and fro,
and not least the failure to recognize the new life that has
come to so many of our congregations through a greater
understanding of, and sharing in the action of, our liturgy.
I hope over the coming decade that it will be possible for the
different rites, both old and new, to be compared with each
other. I hope it will be easier once again to have a Prayer
Book in the home and bring it to church. I hope that a varied
and balanced teaching ministry may be built upon our
Books, both of which reflect a worldwide Anglican face.
Above all, I hope there will be a readiness of people and
priest so to think and plan together about the ordering of
worship that it can lead to freshness of Christian life in
many other areas beside liturgy.

Passionate Coolness

᭢᭢᭢᭢

I AM GLAD that we are celebrating the Festival of the Blessed Virgin Mary in this cathedral[1] where devotion to Mary has been strong throughout the centuries, even when such devotion was out of fashion. In the 1620s, John Cosin – later Bishop of Durham – scandalized some of his contemporaries by renewing the old ceremony of burning candles to the honour of our Lady. 'He busied himself from two of the clock in the afternoon 'til four, climbing long ladders to stick up wax candles.' In this very cathedral the number of candles burned that evening was 220, besides sixteen torches.

All generations have called her blessed and I believe that Mary can be an emblem and an inspiration to us in the future as the Anglican Communion journeys into the second millennium. A meeting like this, the fifth of the Anglican Consultative Council, is inevitably full of house-keeping matters, but I am glad to see from the agenda that the visionary element has not been submerged beneath managerial needs. Every age is one of decision and crisis and this one is no different. The Church is always under judgement. It is always necessary to ask the question, 'Is the face of the Church turned towards her master, Jesus Christ, or is she preoccupied with her status and survival?' This question is one that should concern us as members of the worldwide Anglican Communion in a very special way.

We have never claimed to be the one true Church, to the exclusion of every other Christian Church. We are part of the one, holy, catholic and apostolic Church throughout the world – a Church, now sadly in fragments, which exists only in parts and whose energies are dissipated by unbrotherly conflict. It is our vocation as Anglicans to seek

---

[1] Sermon preached in Durham Cathedral on the occasion of the fifth meeting of the Anglican Consultative Council, 8 September 1981

our own extinction by working for the restoration of the one great universal Church – the coming Church, which Christ promised not even the gates of hell could withstand. We must regularly judge the life of our Churches by this standard – are we working for Christ's coming Church? Are we, like Mary, keeping the things of Jesus and pondering them in our hearts, or are we busy planning for a secure future, like the managers of any other long-established enterprise? This meeting will be reviewing the astonishing progress made in twelve years of consultations between the Anglican Communion and the Roman Catholic Church. I hail this work as a sign that we have not entirely forgotten our vocation, whatever might be said about our complacency as a Church in other respects.

It may be that in some parts of the world we should be serving best by ceasing to exist in separation and instead should attempt to strengthen other Christian bodies, better equipped to represent our Lord in a particular locality. That must be a real question for us in the next two decades, but at present I believe that the example of Mary gives us a clue to a way of serving Jesus Christ which has been cherished in the Anglican tradition and which, I believe, the world particularly needs now. I see in Mary and in the best Anglicans a *passionate coolness*. That sounds like a paradox and you deserve an explanation.

Passionate coolness – certainly we need passion: how is it possible to be a Christian, to love God and his works and to see his finest creation, men and women, so starved that their brains shrivel, without passion? Who could view the spectacle of a world devoting its best talents and a large proportion of its resources to the production of weapons of mass destruction, without passion? Who could witness men and women, God's masterpieces, belittled and under-valued because of their skin colour or sex, without passion?

Passion, however, is not enough. It can be merely destructive, adding to the din and obstructing progress. Self-righteous indignation is an opium which makes people unfit for useful work. Some people are shouting so loudly that they have made themselves deaf. They have made the world a more dangerous and less hopeful place. We need to yoke passion, an urgent desire for change, with cool thought and attention. Passion needs to be married to the receptivity shown by Mary as she kept the signs and sayings about Jesus and pondered them in her heart. The young have given the word 'cool' a positive dimension. Someone who is cool is emancipated from the passions which sway the crowd, from the strident slogans and half-truths which drive out thought and reflection. The cool man is sufficiently collected to observe, to discriminate and to receive a fuller vision of the truth and to put his energies into purposeful and well-considered action. At a time when our airwaves are choked with hateful propaganda, we need this kind of coolness. At a time when some, even in the Christian Church, wish to stop their ears to the clamour of a distressed and threatening world by opting for mindlessness and joining one of the many cults of unreason, we need, in our own Communion, to speak and stand for this kind of reasonable coolness.

This coolness, which we must learn from Mary, is not, however, a matter of mere disengagement – a self-indulgent idling in neutral – it is passionate coolness. It is practised, first to free us from the narcotic fumes of self-induced frenzy and then to allow us to pay attention to God and to act in his strength. 'Behold the handmaid of the Lord – be it unto me according to thy word.' Mary was there to be found by God: she was free to listen to his angel, to receive and obey his word. The Church will never do breathtaking things; will never be able to spend itself in bringing healing and peace to the world, unless it is so deeply attentive to God that his word and life flow into our very veins and direct our hands. Passionate coolness is one way to be free enough to hear God and to share his life.

Our Anglican Communion is sometimes mocked for its stately liturgy, for solemn services like this one, for our emphasis on learning and suspicion of rhetoric. It is true that this tradition can produce dull and complacent churches but, at its best, Anglicanism has exhibited this passionate coolness that we see in Mary. I believe that we need to cherish and deepen our practice of this way of approaching God as part of our contribution to the great Christian centuries to come.

I recently made a hugely enjoyable visit to the Episcopal Church in the United States and made many friends. One of those who made the deepest impression on me was the Dean of the Seminary in the University of the South – Terry Holmes. His tragically early death last month, on the Feast of the Transfiguration, was a shock to the great army of his friends. He personified passionate coolness. He was a patient and careful scholar, a crusader against mindlessness, but he was also fired with a passionate determination to attend to God and to build a Church more expressive of God's word and life. The best tribute to this great Anglican would be to cherish the way of passionate coolness. To persevere in it, as Mary herself persevered. At the beginning of the story, we find her ready to respond to God – 'Be it unto me according to thy word' – pondering signs and sayings in her heart, as she sought to understand and do God's will. This was her way to the end – to the passion and resurrection of her son. It was a way she followed in the din and turmoil of the first Holy Week. The streets were full of shouting crowds. Religious leaders were rushing hither and thither to meetings. The city was full of soldiers, clashing their spears, but it was Mary, silent and still, who remained closest to the Lord. Let her be an inspiration to us.

'Holy Mary, full of grace, the Lord is with thee. Blessed art thou among women and blessed is the fruit of thy womb, Jesus.'

Belief and Witness

🔲🔲🔲🔲

WHEN MY SIXTH-CENTURY predecessor, St Augustine, met the Welsh bishops,[1] he did not show them proper respect. Bede tells us that the Welsh party had been instructed by a hermit that if the Archbishop rose from his seat and greeted them, then 'you will know that he is a servant of Christ and will listen to him obediently. But if he despises you and is not willing to rise in your presence you should despise him in return'. St Augustine did in fact remain seated as they arrived and 'when they saw this they forthwith became enraged and setting him down as a proud man strove to contradict everything he said'. I wish to avoid a similar error. Although our stories were intertwined for 700 years when Wales was an integral part of the province of Canterbury, I come more conscious of my ignorance of the inner quality of church life in Wales than ambitious to sit in the seat of a teacher.

It is vital that we do keep in touch, not only because of our common history, but also because of our common membership of the worldwide Anglican Communion. The Church of England is apt to forget more easily than most that we belong to a world family of Christians in which we are helped to overcome the limitations of vision and understanding which come from living in a particular place and culture, by being able to correct our partial view by reference to the experience of other Christians in very different circumstances. This has been one of the most hopeful developments of the last two decades as we have received teams of preachers from the Church in Uganda and experienced the excitement of being in communion with some of the exuberant and joyful churches of Africa or the flourishing and vigorous churches of Hong Kong and Singapore. Your Archbishop Gwilym has been among

[1] Address to the governing body of the Church in Wales, 14 September 1982

the communion-builders, particularly by his service on the Anglican Consultative Council, which helps to bind us together.

I have received an astonishing education myself over the past two years in the diversity of Anglicanism worldwide, but in the midst of visits to Nigeria and Burma and other rather exotic places it would be a tragedy if the Church of England lost touch with her beloved sister Church in Wales. So many people look to Wales in hope. For people like Jan Morris Wales is a symbol of the community built on a human scale, intimate with nature, cherishing the virtues of the home and farm – a great contrast to the imperial glories of, for example, Venice, which used to fascinate her. In my own cathedral in Canterbury I have a canon, Donald Allchin, who, although not of Welsh origin, has set himself to learn the language because he believes that British culture can be refreshed from that spring. He and many others have Euros Bowen and R. S. Thomas as their bards and we do not need to be told that the Church in Wales is far from being a body of ecclesiastical carpet-baggers but is Welsh to the core. Once again we owe much to Archbishop Gwilym and to this assertion of the Welshness of the Church which has been one of the themes of his entire ministry.

It is only if you cherish your identity and love your roots that you will have something to give to enrich the worldwide communion. We need you to insist on your identity and I want to suggest that this is a profoundly Anglican view. In England in the sixteenth century we began to worship God in our own language and, while not abandoning our desire to be part of a universal Church, true to Scripture and primitive tradition, we developed our own English customs and autonomy. Alas, at the same time in Wales, the Reformation often went hand in hand with an attempt to impose the English language and Englishness. If we are being true, however, to our original inspiration, Anglicans should rejoice at worship with an authentically Welsh flavour. Unless a person or a Church cherishes their identity, they will have nothing to give. But like all God's gifts, your inheritance is to be shared. Proper insistence on identity in the Church of Wales should not degenerate into a selfish ghetto life where talents rust in that compound of inactivity, complacency and fear which characterizes the ghetto.

The sharing of your gifts is not, of course, something for the Anglican Communion alone, but also has implications for your life within Wales. I know that, with the confidence born of a proper assertion of your Welsh identity, after the crisis of disestablishment you have, unlike the Church of England, pressed forward into a covenant relationship with some of the major free churches in Wales. I am well briefed enough to know that there are important differences between your covenant scheme and ours – no immediate mutual recognition of ministries, for example, nor such an ambitious commitment to joint decision-making; but I applaud the progress you have made, particularly in the provision of an order for joint celebrations of the Eucharist. I hope that this will contribute to an atmosphere in which there is real progress locally, in husbanding our resources of manpower, of buildings and cement so that together we can speak and act more effectively for our Lord and be more efficient stewards of what God has given us.

The past few centuries have seen a tragic waste of Christian energy in unchristian feuding between the Churches. In the face of the darkness which confronts faith, we dare not continue in our wasteful and myopic ways. I look forward to hearing about local progress in translating aspirations for unity unto the common coin of practical co-operation because I believe that nothing is real unless it is local. Even with the unhappy failure of the covenant proposals in England, we have a similar task to ensure that pressure is maintained locally to encourage small-scale but none the less significant schemes for practical ecumenical co-operation. I am glad to say that in very many places free-church leaders are showing a willingness to make progress wherever it is possible when they might with some justification have retreated into resentful disappointment.

But of course Christian unity is not the only item on your agenda as a Church. Like the Church of England you are considering how best to respond to the problems and opportunities created by the declining numbers of full-time stipendiary clergy. One clear implication of this is the fostering of a greater sense of partnership between clergy and laity in the essential task of interpreting Christ's teaching for our own time and communicating his presence. The idea still lingers that it is the vicar's job alone to spread and communicate the Christian faith, but he must of course be supported by people who can often penetrate places of work in the factory, school or social services departments where the vicar can only be an amateur and an outsider. The faithful will need more training if they are to discharge these new responsibilities. The most exciting development in the diocese when I was Bishop of St Albans was undoubtedly the Ministerial Training Scheme where men in training for the ordained ministry, men and women who wanted to become readers and lay people who simply wanted to be more articulate in presenting their faith, studied together. Each candidate was, and is still – because the scheme continues to flourish even though the Shepherd has been translated – each candidate is associated with a panel of supporters and in this way the subject of Christian ministry becomes more of a talking-point in the parishes.

In much of the talk of training and how to communicate the faith, the accent seems to be put on technique. If only we used the media properly. If only we made our liturgy more lively. If only we followed some method of evangelism – then church growth would be achieved. I am sceptical about this emphasis on techniques of communication when for a large part of the Church there is a confusion about the central Christian affirmations. We have passed through a necessary period of examination and the qualifying of crude dogmatic statements. The time has come however, when even to intelligent and sympathetic outside observers, the usual voice of our Church seems to be bewilderingly ambiguous and woolly. Someone said to me the other day that there was very little basis on which one could reject any Anglican teaching; and this has closed off one of the ways in which peoples grow at various points in their lives. Even those in rebellion against the Church want something to rebel against and feel cheated, I think rightly, if it is denied them.

An example of this sort of thing was afforded by a
television discussion some years ago on sex and the
teenager. There was the usual panel – a clergyman, a
consultant psychiatrist and a young and very attractive girl
chairperson, who pressed them to define the Church's
attitude to extra-marital intercourse. No kind of principle
emerged from the discussions. It all depends, the panel
said. One must be guided by love. One must be sensitive to
all aspects of the concrete situation. We must be concerned
with the quality of personal relationships. The Church is
failing in its duty if it does not attempt to formulate general
principles in today's circumstances. People are not commonly
in a position to engage in the kind of reflection recom-
mended by the panel when they are in the immediate
presence of temptation or some serious moral crisis.

The problem of many who speak on faith is not so much
how to communicate, but the need for clearer thinking
about what they have to communicate. So often what is
paraded is too simple to be true or too complicated to be
communicated. There have been points in the history of
the Church and theology when the accent was rightly on
qualifications, on the exceptions, on pointing out the
difficulties of maintaining absolute norms; but at present I
believe we have reached the stage when faithful church
people are not sufficiently steeped in gospel perspectives
and the Christian tradition for us to make this critical and
qualifying emphasis the priority. This is true not only of
the laity. I have sometimes been horrified by the casual
attitude I have encountered among the clergy towards
their obligation to work for some theological clarity and
precision. I visited a parish recently and discovered a
sensible vicar, who has a thoroughly good record of work
on large housing estates, in despair about his curate. The
man concerned had emerged from college with an *aegrotat*
and then had been permitted to spend only one year at
theological college before being ordained. He appeared to
his vicar to be a typical case of someone who had been
convinced that the theological quest was of very little
significance in comparison with being a caring and sensitive
pastor. People without a theological cutting edge and with
no clear sense of direction get ground down on housing

estates and this process was already well developed.

So if you were to ask me where I think the emphasis should be in the next few years as we consider the question of what the Church is for, how it ought to conduct its mission and how its manpower should be trained and deployed, I would say that the first priority is to strengthen church members of all kinds in a gospel way of looking at the world and of living their own lives. The accent should be on rigorous theological study at college and on positive and affirmative Christian teaching in our congregations. Of course, one cannot behave as if the critical work of recent decades had never happened. In telling the story of our faith we need to recognize that modern man tends to see it as just one element in the story of mankind on this earth. That creates problems of belief for people. In laying down ethical rules in particular, we need to recognize that we have much greater power to change what was once thought to be part of the 'givenness' of the universe. The availability of contraception, for example, has undoubtedly had an influence on how we evaluate the sexual relationship in marriage. All this calls for a good deal of clear thinking.

It has never been the Anglican way to embrace the strident fundamentalism which takes dangerous short-cuts to security. The cure for Christian confusion is not world-despising dogmatism, or an unchristian over-confidence in our own strength and understanding. But some of those who are attracted to the Christian faith might be forgiven for sometimes thinking that my own Church, the Church of England, has in some part lost touch with the joy and the positive affirmation of the gospel. Too often we have been immobilized by a sense of the complexity of things and a cloud of conflicting witnesses has concealed things which have never been more obvious to eyes which have been opened by Christ. In the world around us and inside us, fear and selfishness are the enemies and we do have a word and a way of life to overcome them. Fear and selfishness can only be overcome by the love of God and by trust in Christ. The best way in which we can help the world now is not by being conformed to its own self-doubt and confusion, but by humbly turning to explore and value the traditional faith.

We have a particular opportunity now at a time in both our Churches of liturgical consolidation. There has, however, been a cost. Perhaps part of the reason why the present generation is less alert to the gospel resonances than any previous one is because of the plethora of liturgies and of translations of the Bible. Now is the time once again to concentrate on steeping the Church in the gospel perspective and restoring phrases to people's minds which will illuminate their everyday experiences. We shall be impoverished indeed if we have moved away from the old Bible and Prayer Book phrases and have nothing which can take their place. So first of all we need to work away at clarity in belief. Whereas when I was head of a theological college in the 1960s I used to say that a mark of a good vicar was that he asked the right questions, now I want to go further and say that he ought to be working hard at providing clear teaching as well. But along with this goes the call for genuineness, the call for the life of a Church or an individual to be aligned to the faith that they declare. Christian discipline is living consistently with your fundamental convictions. In days when words have become threadbare with too much communication, people are inclined to say, 'don't tell me – show me'.

So clarity of thought about our faith and genuineness about our witness should lead to assemblies and governing bodies which are prepared to grasp some nettles. Too often in the Church of England the reports presented to our Synod do not lead to any action but simply to pleas for further study. It would be more constructive if we were prepared to accept or reject some recommendations and were even prepared to make some mistakes. The Church cannot expect to learn from its mistakes unless it is bold enough to make some. Newman, while he was still an Anglican, wrote some sharp words which we might well ponder:

> In the present day, mistiness is the mother of wisdom. A man who can set down half a dozen general propositions which escape from destroying one another by being diluted into truisms, . . . who never enunciates the truth without guarding himself against being supposed to exclude the contradictory – who holds that Scripture is the only authority yet that the

Church is to be deferred to; that faith only justifies, yet that it does not justify without works . . .; that bishops are a divine ordinance yet that those who have them not are in the same religious condition as those who have – this is your safe man and the hope of the Church – this is what the Church is said to want: sensible, temperate, sober, well-judging persons to guide it through the channel of no meaning – between the scylla and charybdis of aye and no.

This is a telling thrust, but what both Newman and those whom he criticized failed to understand was that the life of the Church depends neither on a uniformity of view (as Newman wanted) nor upon a nebulous amalgamation of opposites, such as those he delightfully ridiculed were trying to maintain, but upon the interaction of opposite views, the friction between which can continue to exist only if each of us makes up his mind that there are some things which we do believe and some things we do not.

Clarity in belief, genuineness in our common life, and a readiness to grasp a few nettles, to make a few stands, to grow through our successes or our failures – this is the way to enter more deeply into the mystery of the Lordship of Christ and to discover the power of the words of life in the gospel which will give us all we need to overcome the twin threats of fear and selfishness.

Byzantine Conversations

᭤᭤᭤᭤

THE NAME BYZANTIUM[1] is used for a city – now greatly changed so that Osbert Lancaster can describe Istanbul as the most beautifully situated slum in the world – for an empire AD 325 to AD 1453, the longest in European history; and also for a philosophy of life dismissed by Gibbon as 'devious, dark and bureaucratic' but honoured by W. B. Yeats: 'In Byzantium as never before or since in recorded history religious, aesthetic and practical life were one.' When Constantine was proclaimed emperor at York in AD 306 he determined that what Rome stood for, a blend of Greek culture and Roman order, should not die because of the barbarians, and so in 324–5 he moved the capital of the empire from Rome to Constantinople and saw the Christian religion as the faith to hold that empire together. It is not too much to say that Rome had suffered among other things from a crisis of faith – illustrated by Gibbon's description which may have a familiar ring: 'For the common people all religions were equally true. For the philosophers all religions were equally false, and for the magistrates all religions were equally useful.'

The year 325 marked the establishment of the Christian Church. Nowadays those who are hostile to institutional religion are always trying to get behind Constantine to an ideal picture of Christianity as a loosely knit association of charismatic groups of undogmatic leftist saints. Even W. H. Auden suggests this in his well-known gibe, 'When Christians saw their Agape decline/Into a late lunch with Constantine'. But if the Church is to penetrate the world of institutions with Christian insights it must be incarnate among them.

In the fourth century the outlines of Orthodoxy are discernible. They constitute a package which makes up the

---

[1] The Golden Lecture at St Lawrence Jewry Church, 28 January 1982

tradition in which a Christian is to live and move and have his being. There is the Bible. There are the Creeds. There is the shape of the Liturgy. There is the spiritual heroism of the individual monk, hermit or martyr with his ability to dodge forms and see God. There is the ministerial order to constitute proper authority. In this package none can be removed or over accentuated without distortion. Together they fire the development of the Church. It has always been the claim of the Orthodox that they remain true to that original tradition and the subsequent divisions of the Church represent a falling away.

In the fifth century a number of Semitic, or Oriental Churches – Armenian, Copt or Jacobite – dropped off. That gave the Greek language some dominance in subsequent theological definition. Roman independence developed in the West. The West, less dependent on emperors, inherited some of the mystique of Old Rome. So Thomas Hobbes could describe the pope as 'the ghost of the deceased Roman emperor sitting crowned upon the grave thereof'. In the year 800 they crowned their own Roman emperor and constituted what was always regarded by Byzantium as a bastard Roman empire confined to the West and Frankish in character. They took liberties with the Creed – adding words of their own to the clause about the Holy Spirit. Worst of all, the Fourth Crusade, on its way to liberate the Holy Land, turned against Christian Constantinople and plundered it. For an old-fashioned Orthodox the Roman Catholic Church is built on bad history, bad theology and bad behaviour.

The great shake-up at the Reformation has always been regarded as a domestic fall-out in the heretical West. So, to put it sharply, it was not surprising to hear a simple Orthodox monk at Athos state that a Christian Scientist is a kind of eccentric Roman Catholic.

One of Byzantium's greatest achievements was the civilizing influence it exerted over the people it encountered, and particularly in the conversion of the Slavs in the eleventh century. A Byzantium monk, Cyril, evolved a Slavic alphabet, based on Greek and called the Cyrillic Script, for his missionary work. Areas we now know as Bulgaria and Romania and Russia joined the Orthodox fold and Cyril's written language became in modified form the basis for the culture of the Slav world. The Cyrillic Script and the Orthodox Liturgy have been the guardians of Slav culture.

When in 1453 Constantinople fell to the Turks, South East Europe began to look to Moscow – the Duke of Moscow called himself Caesar or Tsar and the Byzantine two-headed eagle was his emblem; while the Patriarch of Moscow began to be an independent leader of the Orthodox Church. The psychological pull of the Soviet Union today owes not a little to that old claim of Moscow to be the Third Rome.

During the long rule of Islam in the Mediterranean and the Middle East the Orthodox Community, through their traditions, their liturgy, their church buildings, kept alive not only their faith but their cultural identities which might otherwise have become merged in the Islamic empire. Religious leaders became national leaders – ethnarchs as well as hierarchs: an obvious example in our own time would be Makarios. This briefly accounts for the fierce nationalism of the Orthodox Churches, combined with their sense of spiritual unity across national frontiers.

Now it is this Byzantine Church which in the twentieth century has come out of its geographical isolation. In America, by reason of the dispersion, there are Orthodox Churches which are youthful and have much intellectual vigour. In Australia, Melbourne is now the second largest Greek city in the world. In the United Kingdom, the Orthodox Community is arguably the third or fourth largest Christian group. By reason of the Eastern European interest, the Orthodox are claiming a larger place in the World Council of Churches.

The Orthodox Church has had no experience of the Renaissance or the Reformation. It has had no nineteenth-century middle class religious prosperity, which sent missionary movements all over the world, and little experience of the inroads made on Christian thinking through the Rationalist, or Critical, movement.

The Anglican Church has claimed to have a special relationship with the Orthodox. It has tried to keep in touch with a Church that is Catholic but not papal, a

Church that tries to live according to a tradition and does not elevate Bible or biblical fundamentalism or pope. All this had an appeal to the fathers of the Anglican Reformation. It was not, therefore, surprising that the first steps in dialogue with Orthodoxy were made by Anglicans, and the first international conversations, over which I presided, between the whole Orthodox and Anglican worlds began in this country in Oxford in 1973.

It would be idle to deny that those conversations have run into heavy weather, and since that time others started with the Roman Catholic and Lutheran Churches have overtaken them. The Orthodox seem to have discovered that the inroads of modern secularism have been greater in the Anglican Communion than in either the more conservative and politically significant Roman Catholic Church, or the more strongly theological Lutheran. The speculations of Anglican theologians and the ordination of women to the priesthood, as well as the great varieties in our liturgical life, have seemed to the Orthodox not so much to express spiritual vitality as religious St Vitus's dance. For the Anglicans there is a sense that the Orthodox Church is a Church that attempts to live in a world of absolute theological clarity wholly divorced from the realities of intellectual and moral ambiguity in the twentieth century. Again, in days when the record of confrontation between Church and state was impressive in the Lutheran Confessing Church of Germany during the war, and in the Roman Catholic Church in Poland today, there is a question mark over an Orthodox Church which, however heroic some individuals may be, tends to accept the commissar with the same meekness with which it used to accept the minions of the sultan.

It is my contention that these Byzantine Conversations, while they have not realized many of the hopes of those who started them, have nevertheless raised some very important questions, and it is to these that I should now like to draw attention.

To try to unite religious men is to enter a realm where formulas, however momentous, are recognized to be inadequate; where management mergers are wholly superficial; where the attempt to separate theology from history and culture is vain. It is a realm where the heart is engaged as well as the head, a realm where the intangible associations of history and language, shadows and mists, are even more lowering than they are in the life of a nation. As no one can comprehend a nation without knowing much of its history, so no one can understand a Church without its history.

'I see that all your creed is in harmony with mine. I can accept all your doctrinal propositions and you can accept mine – therefore there is nothing to divide us . . .' But does it work like that? The deep-seated half-conscious associations of the past come thrusting in to show that men will not unite, even if they be intellectually agreed. This division cuts deeper into human nature than the top of the mind. It is significant that the most effective endeavours to unite Christians of other denominations have succeeded in countries where Christian history has been short.

A Christian person receives his faith. This faith comes to him in a society, in a way of worship, in a moral imperative. In receiving this faith he does little by way of analysis, little by way of criticism. The mood of faith is humility, and humility bows down before the power which is above its comprehension. The context in which the Christian receives his faith is the total context – a wholeness of religious language, forms of prayer, sacramental life, church order. It thus seems difficult to move into unity without far more growing together in worship and in common life. Without that, unity discussions are dangerously superficial.

Some time ago I visited the Patriarch of Antioch to get him to take our Byzantine Conversations more seriously. He said to me: 'What we need in the Middle East is stability and charity – in my experience theological conversations contribute to neither.' Endless talk and documentation, ceaseless consultations and assemblies, may merely reveal that sharing is not enriching, because the resources are so limited. There is a quotation from St Bernard: 'If you are wise, you will show yourself as a reservoir rather than a canal. A canal spreads abroad water as it receives it, but a reservoir waits until it is filled before overflowing. Thus without loss to itself it communicates its superabundant water.' In the Church of today we have many canals but few reservoirs. So let us have no soft-boiled ecumenism.

The combination in the Byzantine tradition of unity in essentials with fiercely ethnic linguistic and local loyalties forces us Western Christians to look closely at our own attempts to have unity in faith combined with variety in its expression.

In the Roman Catholic Church, the surrender of the Latin language and a degree of collapse in Latin culture over the past two decades, together with liturgical changes and the new confidence of the non-European peoples into whose languages Christian truths need to be baptized, mean that accepting diversity and plurality is a serious problem.

The Anglican Church, on the other hand, has to face the problem of unity within diversity. Roman Catholic and Orthodox critics are inclined to ask what kind of unity they can have with Anglicans, some of whom, and they include professional theologians, seem to believe very little at all. Or they say that the party divisions between Catholic and Protestant are so charged as to negate Anglican unity. If Rome has an authority crisis, Anglicans have an identity crisis. In the past, Anglicans in this country have seen their faith coming through Englishness. In the days of the Empire, we exported Englishness with our Christianity; but now we are attempting to encourage all the parts of the Anglican family to express their faith through the culture and the customs of their part of the world. So our Church in Burma should have a Burmese face, and in Africa an African face. There is an honourable history to this ideal. When Pope Gregory sent Augustine to England and gave him instructions which can still be read in Bede, he said, 'Teach the English the essentials of the faith and if you find customs which are more pleasing than those you have known in Rome, see that they are cherished. For things are not to be loved for the sake of a place, but places are to be loved for the sake of their good things.' It is, however, still a question as to what are the things which hold the Anglican Communion together.

Byzantine Conversations always point up the question of Church/state relations. Both the experience and temperament of the Orthodox Church incline it to divide Caesar's things from God's so far as possible. Few of the nations of Western Europe have known an age when Christianity as such was persecuted. Again, Eastern Europe has known nothing like the medieval papacy. It is very significant that Poland, where confrontation is church policy, has been the most Roman Catholic of Eastern countries. Other dissident nations, like Czechoslovakia and Hungary, have large Protestant populations. The tactics of the Orthodox have been different. Numbered among their saints are diplomats as well as martyrs and mystics.

I remember talking to a Romanian Orthodox bishop. I noticed there were two pictures above his desk – one an icon of the Virgin Mary and the other a large photograph of Mr Ceacesçu, the Romanian president. The bishop saw me glance somewhat surprisedly at the photograph and, shrugging his shoulders, said, 'Ah, Byzantium!' He was expressing the idea that emperors come and emperors go but the Queen of Heaven will remain. Undoubtedly the Orthodox often take the line that they were here before the Turks and Tartars and they were here before the Communists, and they will be here after the Communists have gone. On the way, there will be need for compromise if they are to keep alive the offering of worship, the existence of church buildings and the training of their children through the family tradition. There is the old story of the patriarch of Moscow, about whom it was said that he was frequently asked for thirty pieces of silver and always cheerfully gave twenty-nine.

It is certainly astonishing that in the Soviet Union, after over sixty years of anti-religious propaganda and no religious teaching in schools or provision for it at all in press or broadcasting, the Church remains alive.

In country areas particularly, but also in some of the great cities, it is still nourishing the soul of the people and continuing to throw up from time to time a Solzhenitsyn or a Father Yakunin.

My last, but most significant, point, is that the Byzantine Church is called the Orthodox Church. That is a word which means 'right belief and right worship'. The two hang together and this point follows on the last, since we are inclined to dismiss what happens in church and the character of worship in favour of the gospel of social action or education or political intervention. We need to be reminded that these do not constitute the heart and inspiration of the Christian religion.

At present in the West we are in danger of making our god too small. The neighbourhood god jogging with us along life's way is not the whole truth about the Father of our Lord Jesus Christ. He is a fashionable puppet who fails our imagination as we look into the vast space and ponder the mystery of creation. W. H. Auden, in his play *For the Time Being*, devises a prayer for the worship of such a diminished, comfortable god. 'O God, put away justice and truth for we cannot understand them and do not want them. Eternity would bore us dreadfully. Leave Thy heavens and come down to our earth of waterclocks and hedges. Become our Uncle. Look after Baby, amuse Grandfather, escort Madam to the Opera, help Willy with his home-work, introduce Muriel to a handsome naval officer. Be interesting and weak like us, and we will love you as we love ourselves.' Now that could not ever be said of the sense of eternity which you get in a great act of Orthodox worship. Nor indeed could it be said of the contemplative tradition of the Orthodox mystics and holy men. The emphasis there is that we are fellow pilgrims with all those who have worshipped God in past centuries and who now worship him with clearer vision beyond the grave. We are also fellow pilgrims with the hundreds of millions of Christians alive in the world today who worship the Father on every continent and island. This sense is not optional or a luxury. It is part of a fully mature Christian life. The will to keep in step with our fellow pilgrims saves us from turning our faith into self-indulgent fantasy, a mere endorsement of some national dream, or the desire to preserve some particularly cherished style of life. We depend upon the Church of all the ages and throughout all the world to save us from turning our worship away from the living God to some candy-floss island.

In turbulent and fearful times, when the temptation is to retreat into narrowly based, strident, even fanatical forms of worship, which further divide us from one another and add fuel to the already dangerously combustible state of the world – now more than ever we need to celebrate and cherish our links with the Church of all the ages and throughout the world. The vision of that Church and its achievements gives us hope when present realities hem us in and complexities immobilize us.

There are, then, four considerations which have influenced me in the last twenty years through regular contacts with the Byzantine Church. They are: the difficulty of a Christian tradition being separated from its historical, cultural context in the name of Christian unity; the need to balance universal Christian truths with the local patriotic character; the variety of Church/state relations that Christians are called to follow; the ultimate priority of the spiritual over the social gospel for serious religion. This does not mean that I am unenthusiastic about Christian unity, that I am not proud of Anglican diversity, that I do not applaud the courage of the Poles or admire Protestant independence. Nor do I want to discourage Christians from being change-agents in a society; but Byzantine Conversations remind me that these things are by no means the whole story of Christian witness.

In the second century a Christian author wrote what must be the guiding and uniting aim of us all:

> Christians do not dwell in cities in some place of their own, nor do they use any strange variety of dress or language. They dwell in their own fatherlands as if sojourners in them. They share all things as citizens and suffer all things as strangers. Every foreign country is their fatherland and every fatherland is a foreign country. They obey the appointed laws and they surpass them all in their own lives. To put it shortly, what the soul is in the body, so are Christians in the world.

Rome and Canterbury

⑨⑨⑨⑨

United not Absorbed

JUST OVER FIFTY years ago the bishops of the Anglican Communion saw little hope of unity with Rome.[1] They regretted that Pius XI appeared to contemplate 'complete absorption' (in his encyclical *Mortalium Animos* of 1928) as the only method of achieving unity. The bishops of that 1930 Lambeth Conference were particularly disappointed because the approach of the Malines Conversations had been set aside: that approach had encouraged the Anglican Church to think about being united, not absorbed. At the penultimate Malines Conversation in 1925 Cardinal Mercier had read the paper 'L'Église anglicane unie non absorbée'. It had been prepared by an 'anonymous canonist'. It attracted immediate attention. Some of the details of the paper, now known to have been written by Dom Lambert Beauduin, seem rather fanciful today: his stress on the pallium, a woollen stole blessed by the pope for archbishops, which caused no end of prelatical rivalry in the Middle Ages; his contention that progress towards unity would be wrecked over the question of the precedence of archbishops of Canterbury over cardinals or vice versa – Cardinal Basil Hume and I will not lose much sleep over this. Nor did he really take seriously enough the indigenous English Roman Catholic tradition: on his view the new sees created at and after the restoration of the Roman Catholic hierarchy in 1850 would simply be suppressed.

Yet in spite of serious flaws – which were seen by the Lambeth Fathers in 1930 – the paper remains significant, because it is the first clear recognition that the Churches of the Anglican Communion are bound to seek a unity which respects their autonomous tradition. It is a first systematic essay on the *kind* of unity Rome and Canterbury seek. The

[1] Lenten address at Westminster Abbey, 11 March 1981

nineteenth-century debate had focused on 'Anglican Orders'. In the eighteenth century an archbishop of Canterbury thought of a union with an *Independent* Gallican Church. In the sixteenth and seventeenth centuries both sides saw unity in terms of the Crown imposing a statutory uniformity. So, in spite of its oversimplifications, Beauduin's essay makes its point: we cannot tolerate an Anglican Church *separated* from Rome and we cannot tolerate an Anglican Church *absorbed* by Rome: the Anglican Church, united not absorbed.

Unity and Diversity

However, once this is admitted as a fruitful approach (and such an approach was publicly endorsed by the late Pope Paul VI more than once) an immediate question arises: what range of diversity is compatible with unity or, to put the matter another way, what are the limits of acceptable diversity? The question has to be asked in *any* ecumenical discussion. It is a particularly pressing question for any Church in dialogue with Rome because of the Roman tendency towards an authoritarian centralization and uniformity. Forgive me for making this point somewhat crudely.

The character and model of the Church in the dominant Roman tradition owes a great deal to its origins and location in the centre of a great empire. Many of the detailed administrative practices, legal systems and even archives survived to mould the minds of the architects of the original papal monarchy. The tendency of such an order is to favour a stable ideology, both communicated and enforced by a bureaucracy functioning according to juridical models.

The precondition of the system was the Latin language which became even more useful to the Roman curia after it had died as a living language. An ideological stability is easier to maintain through the medium of a fixed language. The changes in living languages are always subversive to unchanging theological definitions – words do not only change their meaning in a living language, they also change their resonances and their place in a cultural economy.

The collapse of the Latin culture over the past two decades, the liturgical changes within the Roman Catholic Church, the new confidence of the non-European cultures into whose languages Christian truth needs to be baptized – all mean that the problem of perceiving unity in inescapable diversity is not a pressing one for the Roman Church which for so long had been able to fend off the difficulty by reducing diversity to matters of ornament and detail. The Anglican Church had to face the problems of serious diversity, but the Roman Church had to face problems of unity.

Not surprisingly, we have both been having a hard look together at the New Testament and the early Church.

The New Testament

But once we examine the New Testament – or listen to the siren voices of New Testament scholarship – we are confronted by an immediate and serious problem. There is no *one* New Testament picture of anything. To put it bluntly, we are presented with such a bewildering diversity that we begin to doubt whether the concept of unity may not be a reading back of later Orthodoxy. Indeed, the German New Testament specialist Ernst Käsemann writes as follows: 'The New Testament Canon does not, as such, constitute the foundation of the unity of the Church. On the contrary, as such, it provides the basis for the multiplicity of the Confessions.' What, then, can the New Testament teach us about unity in diversity?

Let me take the most important example of New Testament diversity – the clash between Jewish and Hellenistic Christianity, the first serious threat to the unity of the Church. Some of the New Testament documents, notably St Matthew's gospel and the Epistle of St James, strongly affirm the *continuing* validity of the Law of Moses and reject the teaching of St Paul. You will remember that it is in St Matthew that not one 'jot or tittle' of the law will disappear (Matt. 5.17–19) and that Luther found James' treatment of the Pauline doctrine of justification by faith so unacceptable that he branded his letter an 'Epistle of straw'. Indeed, Jewish Christianity in the New Testament

looks very much like what later became the heretical
Jewish Christian sects, for example the Ebionites.

At the other end of the New Testament spectrum,
specially in St Paul and St John, we find a certain
speculative interaction with the philosophical theology of
Hellenistic society. In St John's Gospel in particular we see
a recurring contrast between light and darkness, above and
below, spirit and flesh, which is typical of Hellenistic
dualism and characteristic of the later Gnostic syncre-
tism.

Yet in spite of this very sharp diversity, a profound unity
can also be discerned between Jewish and Hellenistic
Christianity: that unity is the developing understanding of
Christ himself. Jewish Christianity in the New Testament
was already moving away from a *purely* Jewish understanding of Christ. Jesus in St Matthew's Gospel is the
Messiah, 'the Son of the Living God' (16.15–17) and the
birth narrative excludes an understanding of Jesus merely
in terms of being a 'prophet'. In Hellenistic Christianity
Paul preaches an uncongenial *'crucified* Christ' (cf. 1 Cor.
2.1–5) and John insists that the World has become *'flesh'*
(1.14). However contrasting their expressions, Jewish and
Hellenistic Christianity were fundamentally united in
their identification of the *crucified* Jesus with the *exalted* Lord
and this identification lies behind the earliest christological
titles, in whichever Christian milieu they have their origin:
Messiah; Son of Man; Son of God; Lord.

Donald MacKinnon, using different examples of diversity,
once summed up the basic unity of the New Testament like
this: 'We cannot conjure the Jesus of Luke out of the Jesus
of Mark, but we can see standing behind them both,
shaping, controlling and even twisting their narratives, the
sure hand of the one they strive to bear witness to in the
fellowship of the Spirit.'

The Early Church

When we turn to the early Church we have the impression
that instead of looking for unity in diversity we are now
looking for diversity in unity. From the point of view of the
emergent Great Church, Fathers and heretics could be

neatly separated – dad and cads, as G. L. Prestige used to say. Schism was not *in* the Church but *out* of it.

The question is now not how much diversity can be found in a general study of early Christian history but how much diversity can be found within the undivided communion of the Great Church of the first centuries. This appeal must not be uncritical, as if there were no divisions, no schisms, and all was sweetness and light. But no church historian could think that. Yet there is still a certain cogency in speaking of the undivided Church, whether one draws a line at the separation of the Oriental Churches from Byzantine Orthodoxy (a schism between Greek-speaking and Semitic-speaking Churches), or the later division between Rome and Constantinople (where language and culture again played their part in the cleavage between the Greek and Latin Churches). The point of an appeal to an 'undivided tradition', however defined, is that once any Christian tradition develops an isolation from the wider Church its doctrine and life begin to be less than fully catholic – according to the whole.

What can we learn about diversity in unity from the early and undivided tradition of the Catholic Church? I do not want to offer purely liturgical or even disciplinary examples, even though disputes about new liturgies in both Churches raise a lot of steam and marriage discipline or clerical celibacy touches even more sensitive areas. The real issue, however, is the problem of theological and doctrinal pluralism. Was, and is, it possible to have unity in faith and difference in its expression?

This question was posed in its sharpest way for the early Church in the christological dispute between Antioch and Alexandria in the fifth century. At the risk of over-simplification: Alexandrine Christology stressed the unity of the incarnate Christ; Antiochene Christology stressed the reality of Jesus' humanity and so saw a distinction in the incarnate Lord. The Council of Chalcedon was a proper compromise which sought to do justice to the insights of both schools: *one* person in *two* natures. But the disputes before and after the Council were more than usually influenced by personalities and ecclesiastical empire-building.

Even so, just before the Council we have a very

significant recognition of theological and even doctrinal
pluralism in one communion. In 433 two of the major
protagonists, Cyril of Alexandria and John of Antioch,
exchanged remarkable letters. John wrote to Cyril and sent
him his confession of faith. Though the letter was irenic, it
contained the normal Antiochene theology of the 'two
natures' of Christ – directed explicitly against Cyril's 'one
nature'; but at the same time John clearly stated the unity
of the 'person' of Christ and the consequent legitimacy of
describing Mary as 'Mother of God'. Cyril, a real hard-liner
and no woolly-minded ecumenist, replied with great
generosity and rejoiced that they shared a common faith
and his reply was canonized by the Council fourteen years
later. As Fr Emmanuel Lanne puts it, Cyril 'accepted a
profession of faith in which the theological perspective was
not his own'.

Another example, of a different kind, which is actually
found in the Creed, shows the early Church quite prepared
to be reticent in defining the faith for the sake of unity.
One of the reasons for convening the Council of Constantinople in 281 (we celebrate its sixteenth hundredth
anniversary this year) was to settle the disputed status of
the Holy Spirit. Was the Holy Spirit a creature, or, on the
contrary, like the Son, of the same 'substance' as the Father
and so properly to be called God? The majority of the
Council were clear enough that the Holy Spirit was indeed
'of one being' with the Father and many were happy to go
on and say he was God. Yet the form accepted and which
we still use in the Creed was much more reticent: 'We
believe in the Holy Spirit, the Lord, the Giver of life, who
proceeds from the Father. With the Father and the Son he
is worshipped and glorified. He has spoken through the
Prophets.' This cautious phraseology accords very much
with the teaching and 'ecumenical' sensitivity of St Basil
the Great. Basil was concerned to defend the legitimacy of
the Church's worship of the Spirit, but – in John Kelly's
phrase – he 'practised diplomatic caution' in his actual
language about the Spirit.

Once again different ways of expressing the faith, even
in so central a matter as the divinity of the Holy Spirit, are
compatible with unity.

Anglican Comprehensiveness

The point of our exploration of these aspects of the unity and diversity of the New Testament and the early Church has been to show that, far from being incompatible with unity, a very wide diversity is found among the earliest Christian communities and that, even when the Church developed its structures in a more unified way in the centuries which followed, this did not necessarily entail the acceptance of identical expressions of faith. In now going on to speak of Anglican comprehensiveness I do not wish to insinuate that the Anglican tradition is the direct or only heir to the primitive Church. Nor do I want to suggest that Anglican comprehensiveness is the only possible way of achieving unity in diversity presented to us by the Church of the New Testament, and the Fathers may put Anglican comprehensiveness, when rightly understood, in a more favourable light, as well as indicating the range of diversity feasible in any Anglican/Roman Catholic union.

At the English Reformation a number of forces were at work. There was a new nationalism and a 'godly prince' to embody it. There was the desire for vernacular Scriptures and Liturgy. There was the influence of the continental Reformation, at first Lutheran but later Calvinistic. And there was a wish by many to preserve a continuity with the Church of the previous centuries. The Elizabethan Settlement was a more or less conscious attempt to comprehend within the Church of England all those who would accept the Scriptures, the Creeds, the Sacraments of Baptism and the Eucharist, a liturgy and the threefold ministry of bishops, priests and deacons. To achieve this comprehension it was absolutely necessary to make a clear distinction between fundamentals and non-fundamentals – a distinction probably taken from the 'ecumenical' Lutheran reformer Melancthon. The clearest expression of this distinction is found as recently as the 1968 Lambeth Conference: 'Comprehensiveness demands agreement on fundamentals, while tolerating disagreement on matters in which the Church may differ without feeling the necessity of breaking communion.'

Yet immediately the distinction is made, an urgent

question arises: where is the line to be drawn? At the close of the sixteenth century and during the seventeenth century, in the polemic with both Puritans and Recusants, the classical Anglican answer to this question emerged. The answer gave Anglicanism its distinctive ethos. It had three characteristics.

First, that the common Reformed appeal to Scripture was tempered by the role of tradition, not, of course, as an additional source of revelation, but as a sure guide to the uncertainties of scriptural interpretation. As a result of this, the study of the Fathers had great importance – with the interesting result that eventually the doctrine of the incarnation became more central to mainstream Anglicanism than justification by faith.

Next, that there was an appeal to reason which reflected the assurance of Renaissance humanism – an appeal powerfully developed by Richard Hooker and others. The Enlightenment, too, eventually became a characteristic of Anglican thought.

Finally, that doctrine was presented in the liturgical worship of the Church. The *lex orandi* was the guide to the *lex credendi*. Unlike other Reformed Churches, the Prayer Book was a formula of faith.

Now these three characteristics were, and are, by no means exclusively Anglican, but their particular combination gave Anglican theology, spirituality and pastoral practice its distinctive stamp. They gave Anglicanism not so much a distinctive theological content as a distinctive theological method. Hence, Richard Hooker wrote about methodology and precisely entitled it *Of the Laws of Ecclesiastical Polity*. He did not write a systematic *Summa* or an Anglican version of John Calvin's *Institutes*.

'In the mind of an Anglican, comprehensiveness is not compromise' – so said the 1968 Lambeth Conference. Rightly understood, it is the achievement of unity in diversity through the distinction of the essential from the non-essential by means of the holy Scriptures interpreted by tradition, in the light of reason, all expressed in and through the corporate worship of the Church.

Criticisms

In suggesting that Anglican comprehensiveness (and the distinction between fundamentals and non-fundamentals it entails) is a legitimate way of expressing the unity in diversity we find in the New Testament and the early Church, I am aware of a vulnerability to sharp criticism. Yes, a Roman Catholic or Orthodox critic will say, it sounds all right but it is a *paper* system – what kind of unity can we have with Anglicans, some of whom, and they include some professional teachers of theology, seem to believe nothing at all? Or it will be said that the party strife in the Church of England between 'catholic', 'evangelical' and 'liberal' is so sharp as to negate internal Anglican unity, let alone unity with Rome.

The first thing to point out is that Anglicans themselves make similar self-criticisms. Professor Stephen Sykes's important book *The Integrity of Anglicanism* is on target here.

Second, 'abuse does not take away the use of a thing' – a remark which seventeenth-century Anglicans were always addressing to the Puritans. There are some Anglicans who seem to be saying that there are no fundamentals at all, or rather, that one can never be certain what they are. Anglicanism depends, on the contrary, on the possibility of a public distinction between essentials of faith and non-essentials being made and embodied in the worship of the Church. To refuse to draw the line anywhere or to draw it in a highly personal and idiosyncratic way is in fact to abandon the classical Anglican method I have described. Now I have no wish to be oversimplistic: it is obvious to all Christians that there is a general crisis of doctrinal authority. The crisis has arisen for many reasons, but not least because of the acceptance of biblical citicism – and we can do no other. There is also a growing realization that some degree of 'doctrinal' or credal criticism also has to be accepted. Add to these the contemporary lack of trust in human reason and the seventeenth-century Anglican appeal to Scripture, tradition and reason looks less secure. I am not a classical Anglican fundamentalist and want no witch hunts. To quote the 1968 Lambeth Conference again: 'Comprehensiveness implies a willingness to allow liberty of interpretation, with a certain slowness in arresting or restraining exploratory thinking.'

Third, in spite of some impressions to the contrary, comprehensiveness does not imply that plain contradiction can be a normal expression of Anglican diversity. Stephen Sykes has suggested that from the latter part of the nineteenth century, aided and abetted by F. D. Maurice, comprehensiveness has come to be thought of in almost Hegelian terms: Catholic thesis, Protestant antithesis and Anglican synthesis. No doubt there is a real truth in the idea of 'a continuing search for the whole truth' in which Protestant and Catholic emphases 'will find complete reconciliation' (Lambeth Conference 1968). But this idea has to be recognized as a modern one. It is quite alien to original Anglican thought that there could be logically opposite expressions of faith in fundamentals. To be an Anglican is not to be content with self-contradiction.

Lastly, comprehensiveness, properly understood as the distinction between fundamentals and non-fundamentals, will be seen to be not unrelated to the doctrine of the 'hierarchy of truths', canonized by the Second Vatican Council, the implications of which have not yet been fully worked out.

Questions for the Future

I began with the idea of the Anglican Church united not absorbed. In the light of my very Anglican appeal to Scripture and the early Church, and of my attempt to relate Anglican comprehensiveness to the unity and diversity I believe we find there, I want to conclude by suggesting some questions Anglicans should now be asking Roman Catholics in order to elucidate what unity not absorption would mean.

Some hard questions must be asked about Vatican centralization. As early as the close of the second century, Pope Victor was threatening the excommunication of the whole of the Asian episcopate because they kept Easter on a different date from the West. Fortunately Irenaeus put him right. But the tendency to uniformity still seems to be a Roman attitude of mind (for the reasons I mentioned earlier). The Uniat Churches in the USA are forbidden the married clergy they have had from time out of mind in the Middle East because this clashes with 'Latin' canon law. Or, to bring the matter nearer home, how much freedom does the Roman Catholic Episcopal Conference of England and Wales have to pursue moral and pastoral initiatives culturally relevant to the mission of Christ in this country? To put it more directly, would Anglicans be expected to accept the 'Latin' attitudes and rulings of the various Vatican Congregations? The question is acute when we consider moral issues relating to particular interpretations of natural law and the Anglo-Saxon tradition of the informed Christian conscience.

Ultimately, the theological questions can be put like this: what is involved (and what is *not* involved) in acceptance of the universal ministry of the Bishop of Rome? Is this minstry not solely concerned with the basic unity of the faith in the worldwide communion of the Churches and their God-given diversity? Would this mean, at the most, a form of universal presidency in charity when essential matters of faith are at stake? What relation, then, would the Vatican have to the various Synods of the Anglican Communion? There are, therefore, some questions about the Anglican acceptance of a universal primacy which cannot be answered until Anglicans and Roman Catholics have come to some consensus on what acceptance actually involves.

Beauduin saw something of this even in the 1920s and expressed it in the concluding words of his paper:

> What will Rome think of this plan? It is clear that it suggests a principle of decentralization which is not in accordance with the actual tendencies of the Roman Curia, a principle that could have other applications. Would it not be a good and a great good? Yet would Rome be of this opinion? Nothing can allow us to foresee what would be the answer.

Beauduin did not know how Rome would react to his question. In the 1920s it was, in any case, certainly premature. But we are now at the stage of dialogue where the hard questions need to be put – and Rome will have some tough questions to put to Anglicans as well. In this exchange both traditions will be purified and renewed. Both will have something to give to the other.

In putting a few Anglican questions in the light of the New Testament and the early Church and arguing that Anglican comprehensiveness does not mean Anglicans have no faith, I do not think it will be assumed that I am not absolutely committed to Anglican/Roman Catholic unity. I ask questions precisely because I am, and deeply so, for both personal and theological reasons. It is therefore my profound hope that when the present successor of Pope Gregory comes to this country next year St Augustine's present successor and he will be able to take a step together towards that unity – towards the mutual exchange which will show both traditions more clearly what visible structures that unity in diversity requires.

The Papal Visit

THIS IS A service of celebration,[1] but the present moment is full of pain for so many in the world. Millions are hungry and the sacred gift of life is counted cheap while the nations of the world use some of their best resources and much of their precious store of human ingenuity in refining weapons of death. With so much to celebrate in life and so much work to be done to combat life's enemies, disease and ignorance, energy is being wasted in conflict. Our minds inevitable. The present moment is not empty of hope, but the South Atlantic, and we also remember the sufferings of Your Holiness's own fellow countrymen in Poland. But Christians do not accept hunger, disease and war as inevitable. The present moment is now empty of hope, but waits to be transformed by the power which comes from remembering our beginnings and by the power which comes from a lively vision of the future.

Remembering our beginnings; celebrating our hope for the future; freeing ourselves from cynicism and despair in order to act in the present; it is this style of Christian living which gives shape to this service. Every Christian service contains this element of remembering the beginnings of our community, when our Lord walked this earth. At this season of the year, we particularly remember the gift of the Holy Spirit at the first Pentecost and the sending out of the apostles to carry the faith of Jesus Christ to the furthest ends of the world. We recall one of the first missionary endeavours of the Roman Church, in its efforts to recapture for Christ a Europe overwhelmed by the barbarians. In the year 597, in the words of the English historian, the Venerable Bede, Your Holiness's great predecessor Gregory, prompted by divine inspiration, sent a servant of God named Augustine and several more God-

---

[1] Introductory address, Canterbury Cathedral, 29 May 1982

fearing monks with him to preach the word of God to the English race'. Augustine became the first archbishop of Canterbury, and I rejoice that the successors of Gregory and Augustine stand here today in the church which is built on their partnership in the gospel.

We shall trace and celebrate our beginnings in this service by reaffirming our baptismal vows made at the font at the beginning of our Christian life and by saying together the Creed, an expression of the heart of our common Christian faith, composed in the era before our unhappy division. The emphasis, then, will be on the riches of what we share and upon the existing unity of the Christian Church, which transcends all the political divisions and frontiers imposed upon the human family. One of the gifts Christians have to make to the peace of the world is to live out the unity that has already been given to them in their common love of Christ.

But our unity is not in the past only, but also in the future. We have a common vision, which also breaks up the lazy prejudices and easy assumptions of the present. The Chapel of the Martyrs of the twentieth century is the focus for our celebration of a common vision. We believe even in a world like ours which exalts and applauds self-interest and derides self-sacrifice, that 'the blood of the martyrs shall create the holy places' of the earth. Our own century has seen the creation of ruthless tyrannies by the use of violence and of cynical disregard of truth. We believe that such empires, founded on force and lies, destroy themselves. The kingdom spoken of by our Lord Jesus Christ is built by self-sacrificing love which can even turn places of horror and suffering into signs of hope. We think of Your Holiness's own fellow countryman, the priest Maximilian Kolbe, who died in place of another in the hell of Auschwitz. We remember with gratitude our own brother, Archbishop Janani Luwum in Uganda, who worked in the worst conditions for Christ's kingdom of love and justice and whose death inspires us still and will mark the future more deeply than the lives of his oppressors.

We remember all the martyrs of our century of martyrs, who have confirmed Christ's Church in the conviction that even in the places of horror, the concentration camps and prisons and slums of our world – nothing in all creation can separate us from the active and creative love of God in Jesus Christ our Lord.

If we remember that beginning in Jesus Christ our Lord, if we can face the suffering involved in travelling his way, if we can lift our eyes beyond the historic quarrels which have tragically disfigured Christ's Church and wasted so much Christian energy, then we shall indeed enter a faith worthy of celebration, because it is able to remake our world.

The Covenanting Proposals

◧◧◧◧

'HOW WILL THE Archbishop of Canterbury vote?' was a question that I heard put over the weekend.[1] That has not in recent years finally determined our major decisions as a Church. Naturally I would be less than human if I did not often wish that it did. When I spoke in our last debate, I tried to stir up some enthusiasm and voted in favour of the Proposals. Here, I said, is a chance for us to set an example of how Churches can with integrity be reconciled as a major step forward in our joint mission. Here, I said, we can bring more of English Christianity with us in our dialogue with other world confessional families. There will be short-term difficulties and ambiguities, but if we can cope with these, and reduce some of them, the price will be worth paying. I hold to the same opinions today and will try to tell you why I intend to vote in favour of the motions, even though I remain very sensitive about this question: 'Are you in danger of sacrificing our character as a Church which shares with the great part of Christendom a ministry given by God as a sign of continuity and unity?'

Bishop Lancelot Andrewes touched on today's issues when he spoke to seventeenth-century Presbyterians about episcopal ordination. 'Even if our order be admitted to be of divine authority, it does not follow that without it there can be no salvation or that without it a Church cannot stand. Only a blind man could fail to see Churches standing without it. Only a man of iron could deny that salvation is to be found within them. We are not men of iron of that type.' Coming from the heat of the seventeenth-century debates, those words impress upon us the historic point at which a large part of English Christianity has arrived today in debating these Proposals. Anglicans have

[1] Speech in the debate on the Covenanting Proposals, General Synod, 7 July 1982

consistently claimed that the 'historic episcopate' must be the ministerial basis for unity. The Methodist Church and the United Reformed Church have now officially decided that an episcopally ordered ministry is acceptable in itself and necessary for unity. They may not express their acceptance of episcopacy as boldly as Hooker did when he declared that 'the Church of Christ is and hath been since the beginning governed by bishops having permanent superiority and ruling power'. But then nor would we. Try telling the General Synod it is as at this day governed by the House of Bishops, or indeed (as I have said) the Chairman of the House of Bishops. We have all moved from the slogans and pamphlets of the past to a renewed and convergent understanding of the Church and its ministry in which the episcopal order is seen to focus and express the unity of the Church.

Whatever division of conscience and opinion is found in today's Synods, all Anglicans must be profoundly grateful for this immense stride towards reconciliation. Should the Synod, in the event, not be able to reach sufficient unanimity to go forward, I want to record the absolute necessity of a renewed determination to build on what has so far been achieved. For what is done here will have ramifications wherever we have exported our antique feuds and prejudices. Nevertheless, however momentous the present opportunity is, and however generous our partners have been in the light of their own history, our decision must ultimately have a doctrinal integrity of its own if it is to stand the test of time and to serve the true unity of the Church.

I said last time that I did not expect to see the Proposals back here in precisely the same form as they then were. The Churches' Council for Covenanting responded precisely to my request for more work in three areas. I gratefully acknowledge what has been done, some of which is publicly reflected in the First Progress Report. Yet I also have to admit to a real frustration that procedures, both synodical and ecumenical, do not admit of the sort of changes I hoped to see at this stage. We seem to be servants of procedures rather than making procedures serve unity. In the last debate Colin Buchanan also spoke of the mere inches which separated some on either side of the divide among us, and I believe this is still true.

So what is my chief reservation which I still retain while ready to vote 'Yes' today? Last time the Synod motions specifically spoke of the incorporation of the Free Church ministries 'within the historic ministry of the Catholic Church'. I urged that the Blessing of Presbyteral Ministries must be approached with the explicit intention of such incorporation. This had, of course, already been requested at York in 1978. But this appears to be problematic. The Board for Mission and Unity Report before us makes its response to this issue at paragraph 23, and the Board itself puts the crucial question: 'Why are the actual words used in the General Synod Resolution not used in the Covenant Service?' We are told it is because incorporation obviously does not apply to the Anglican priests present, nor indeed to the Moravian ministers, and furthermore that this would not express the fact that all the ministries have received distinctive gifts of the Spirit which are now to be shared. The Board finally makes the point that it is not the case that Free Church ministers are incorporated into the Church of England. While all this is true, I am bound to say that I still see no reason at all why this presents a clear declaration of intention which at this crucial point would lift the Proposals from what looks like mere mutual recognition after hard bargaining to the truly creative plane which is the characteristic of prayer in the Spirit of Christ. There appears to be a fearful reluctance to contemplate anything other than an absolute reciprocity which savours more of bartering than grace.

Let it first be said in preface, rubric or prayer that we on our part officially recognize the reality of the ministry of Word and Sacrament of the Free Churches, and they on their part ours. But having said this loudly and clearly in such a way that no Free Churchman need feel his ministry impugned, there remains the further step of expressing the incorporation of the acknowledged ministries of the Methodist and Reformed Churches within the historic ministry of the Catholic Church. I believe this can be said sensitively with the humble Anglican recognition that the Catholic ministry is not our private possession and that there is thus no question of covert reception into the Church of England. The importance of the Service of Reconciliation can hardly be overstated. My hope is that it will be marked by an intense but unaffected love of our Christian neighbour. If approached in this way, the service could be transformed into a religious event capable of outflanking theological ambiguities and generating the dynamism to carry us through the necessary period of revising our institutional procedures. If the Service of Reconciliation is not such a religious event, then it will be a judgement on the Churches. Acquiescence is not enough. Covenanting demands people who are enthusiastically committed to it.

The Synod will expect me to offer my views on the ecumenical consequences of accepting the Proposals for our relationships with the Roman Catholic and Orthodox Churches. All that I have so far said had naturally something of this in mind. But the experience of the papal visit did not leave me saying, 'Now let us concentrate exclusively on this wonderful opportunity for Roman Catholic relations', but rather, 'Surely God is telling us that things are possible which we never thought could happen in our day'. In the Common Declaration which I signed with the Pope we affirmed the goal of 'the visible unity of all God's people', and I want to endorse the Board for Mission and Unity's rejection of any suggestion of 'either/ or' tactics. But to speak of the unity of the Ecumenical Movement does not absolve us from the difficult task of making particular decisions. As far as the Roman Catholic Church is concerned, you have the relevant part of Cardinal Hume's address to the Free Church Federal Council before you, and we must not underestimate the force of the traditional Catholic view of the necessity of episcopal ordination. While it is also possible to find Roman Catholic theologians who take a different view, I am sure the Cardinal's personal hesitations will also be shared by many in Rome. Yet on the other side no one can deny that the acceptance of episcopacy by the Free Churches cannot but make the dialogue Rome is already engaged in with those Churches significantly easier. I would like to think that acceptance of the Proposals would bring the Free

Churches into our discussion with Rome so that we can look forward to an ultimate unity which includes all the strands of English Christianity sundered in the sixteenth, seventeenth and eighteenth centuries.

As for the Orthodox, my own discussions with Archbishop Methodios and others lead me to conclude that (as with Rome) there is more diversity than Anglicans sometimes imagine. I believe it would be possible to commend the Proposals favourably to the Orthodox – not least in respect of the Reconciliation of Ministries – if they were strengthened and made explicit in the way I have already suggested. In the earlier debate I quoted one of the Byzantine ordination prayers with its powerful affirmation that the 'Divine Grace always heals what is wounded and makes up what is lacking'. I am told, and Archbishop Methodios gives me authority to quote him, that if we make it clear that we intend the Free Church Ministries shall be part of the threefold catholic ministry, this is true to that 'economy' of the Holy Spirit in the life of the Church. The Orthodox have always had a sense of the greatness of God's love and mercy which allows the Church to go beyond the provisions of Canon Law for the benefit of those who are within the Church or who are coming to be united with it. There are precedents in church history for exceptions to the normal rule.

On the negative side, the acceptance of women ministers presents serious problems for both Rome and Constantinople, which we must not underestimate. While Rome and Constantinople are perfectly aware that some Anglican provinces ordain women, they still regard the Church of England's stance on this matter as important.

But in the end our friends from Rome and Constantinople both tell me that they cannot judge the proposals for us. We have to make up our own minds with the probability that our acceptance of them will create problems – even serious ones – in the immediate years ahead, though ultimately it will facilitate the task of bringing about a much wider unity which will draw together Protestant and Catholic, East and West. We now begin to see the cost of the claim to be a *via media* – a claim we have sometimes made too glibly. I do not myself see the decision as a choice which excludes. I do not believe that our friends in Rome or Orthodoxy will regard our acceptance as a choice to be Protestant. I do see difficulties if the Proposals are not strengthened at the point of Reconciliation. I am prepared to go forward, even with my hesitations, in the trust that things can and will be done. I am only sorry that we have not been able to find the means to make improvements at this stage so that we could have carried more of the Synod and so that I myself could be more enthusiastic.

I must briefly voice my other main reservation. If there is a positive vote, a great deal of work needs to be done in devising procedures for joint decision-making between the Covenanting Churches. We should scrutinize this process closely, referring all that is said and done to one vital test – are we helping the Churches to be more serviceable in presenting the person and teaching of our Lord to those who do not know him? It would be a tragedy if the consequences of Covenanting were to be an increase of ecclesiastical introversion and a protracted series of negotiations at every level of church life, absorbing rather than generating Christian energy. I dread the thought of having to have such negotiations before I could hold an ordination.

In coming to my decision, which has not been easy, I do not want to suggest that those who clearly share some of my difficulties but find they cannot vote for the Proposals with me are somehow lacking in ecumenical commitment or Christian charity. I hope that majorities and minorities will respect each other's decisions without recrimination or rancour. We must recognize that there will be differences in the ecumenical priorities of different members of the Synod, often affected by the local pastoral experience of bishops, priests and laity as well as by their theology. Those whose decision is different from their own have also come to their judgement conscientiously. I hope not many will be voting today because their party says aye or no, or even because I come down just on one side of the watershed. Let each vote be cast according to the lights of each member and let us respect those who walk through a different door from the one we choose.

I close with some words from a former Archbishop of Canterbury, William Wake. At the beginning of the eighteenth century he was at one and the same time conducting an elaborate correspondence with Roman Catholic theologians in France and was also engaged in an equally lengthy discussion with Swiss and German Protestants on the restoration of the historic episcopate. Neither of Wake's proposals came to the difficult point of decision and application which we are at today. But I think that the spirit of today's decision will be his, whether you are filled with enthusiastic conviction, conscientious doubt, or find yourself in between. Writing to a friend about his painstaking work for unity, he realized that he would see no fulfilment in his own lifetime. He went on: 'I may have been otherwise an unprofitable servant, nevertheless I have ever sought, counselled, and with all my zeal and effort pursued those things which belong to the peace of Jerusalem.' The resonances of those words, 'the peace of Jerusalem', must remind us that all our work and prayer for unity have this end – the peace and harmony which come from above to bring into harmony the brothers and sisters of the one God and Father of us all.

The Proposals for a Covenant for unity with the United Reformed, Methodist and Moravian Churches were not accepted by the General Synod. The voting was:

	Ayes	Noes	Abstentions
Bishops	38	11	1
Clergy	148	91	2
Laity	154	71	0

Identity and Integration

🔲🔲🔲🔲

THIS THANKSGIVING SERVICE[1] is my first public act of worship since I celebrated my own silver wedding anniversary at the beginning of this week. So I feel particularly close to you since your history as a Mar Thoma Congregation and my marriage have marched side by side for the last twenty-five years. I see that your history has been marked by a debate about the relative claims of the need to preserve your identity as Mar Thoma Syrian Christians and the desirability of making the full contribution to British society which only a measure of integration can make possible. Some of you, I know, as well as worshipping here also worship in your parish churches. I hope and pray that you will continue to respect both the need to preserve identity and to promote integration.

As a Western Church, we deeply value and give thanks for our communion with one of the most ancient Churches of the East. After the exuberance and self confidence of the nineteenth-century, we have become aware of the imbalance within western culture, our estrangement from the elemental, from mystery and from the world of symbol and intuition. Christ is so much greater than the view any of us have of him. 'God has given him a name which is above every name, that every tongue should confess that Jesus Christ is Lord to the glory of God the Father.' He is to be worshipped by all and, indeed, he is not fully seen or worshipped unless every tongue and all nations bring their own particular gifts to his service. We need you to be true to your identity as Indian Christians in order to add to the richness and breadth of our understanding and worship of Christ. In the nineteenth century you welcomed missionaries from the Church Missionary Society and you gave them an honour-

---

[1] Address at the service for the Mar Thoma Congregation's Silver Jubilee, St Mary's Church, Newington, 10 September 1982

able place in the history of your Church. They had an
influence on the way in which you study and regard the
holy Scriptures. Now we need your gifts. Preserving your
identity as Eastern Christians is not selfish; it is the only
way in which you can enrich your brothers and sisters in
the worldwide communion of Christ's Church.

This is a very Anglican view. In the sixteenth century we
began to worship God in our own language and, while not
abandoning our desire to be part of a universal Church,
true to Scripture and primitive tradition, we developed our
own English customs and autonomy. So it is close to the
heart of the Anglican tradition to insist that the Indian
Christ should have an Indian face, so that he can draw into
himself the riches of every tongue and every culture on
earth. Alas, we have not always been true to our own
tradition. We have sometimes confused the gospel with
Englishness and tried to make Indian Christians into
Europeans.

You have resisted this process and we are grateful that
you have, since now one of the reasons we particularly
rejoice over communion with the Mar Thoma Church is
the evidence that Church provides that Christianity in
India is not some mere colonial import. There were
Christians in Kerala even before the time of the first
Archbishop of Canterbury, St Augustine, who landed in
Kent in 597. The churches that look to St Thomas as their
founder can refute the slur that Christianity in India is a
colonial ideology. You have a special responsibility in
contemporary India to be the face and hands of our Lord, to
make him known and to serve him. 'Ye are my witnesses,
saith the Lord, and my servant whom I have chosen.' You
have this responsibility not only in India, of course, but also
in Britain, 30,000 of whose citizens speak Malayalam. So
we give thanks for your identity, for the way in which you
have preserved the God-given gifts of your Indian heritage.
Unless you cherish your identity you will have nothing to
give. But, like all God's gifts, yours are to be shared. Proper
insistence on identity should not degenerate into a selfish
ghetto life where talents rust in that compound of
inactivity, complacency and fear which characterizes the
ghetto.

The other pole is integration, to desire to make a contribution to the society of which you are a part. 'Let this mind be in you which was also in Christ Jesus who took upon him the form of a servant.' I believe that the Mar Thoma Syrian community has already made a very considerable contribution to the life of this country. We have entered a period where many western people are so uncertain of their own identities and traditions that they are easy prey for spectacular and spurious wise men from the East. There is true wisdom to be found in the East, not least in the ancient Christian Churches, and we look for your help in our joint God-given task to build a world in which every knee shall bow at the name of Jesus.

But you also have a place in the Indian nation, in which the majority of citizens belong to one of the other great world religions. We are only at the beginning of our attempts to understand one another, but the peace of the world depends on all the lovers of God coming to respect each other's beliefs more deeply. There should be no compromise with our loyalties, but there should be a willingness to thank God for the treasures and insights to be found in other religions. Thanksgiving for our own biblical inheritance and thanksgiving for the goodness to be found in the lives of Muslim and Hindu believers is a practical contribution to softening hearts and making the world more in the image of the one who came with the open hand and not with a clenched fist. 'Identity' and 'integration', the two poles of your history as a congregation, are key words which cast light upon much of our life as Christians. I began with a reference to my own silver wedding celebrations and clearly in marriage there has to be a firm hold on personal identity or we have nothing to give in the process of integration as a married couple seeks to become one flesh.

In our relations with God we are not to see ourselves dissolved into some impersonal divine spirit. In the Book of Genesis, Jacob wrestles all night with the angel of the Lord and refuses to submit. As a result, he wins a clearer and more conscious identity as Israel and this new identity, signified by the change of his name from Jacob to Israel, also gives him the potential for a deeper integration with the life of God in more obedient service.

Perhaps there is even a model for the divided Churches of world Christendom here. We must explore as deeply as we can and realize our own individual identities as children of the heavenly Father, who said: 'I have called thee by thy name . . . thou art precious in my sight. I have loved thee.' God loves us individually and gives us gifts as individuals for the purpose of linking us to other people in a community which can reflect more and more of the glory of God. Integration or unity must not be an imposition of one pattern, one tongue, one set of customs. That is to thwart God's work in creating diversity. We must not see integration or unity as a reversion to the undifferentiated, unconscious mass which existed in the beginning, but as an ascent to the integration of marriage – the conscious union of gifts to make a richer whole. It is only after undergoing such a process of integration that we shall see the full glory in the face of Jesus Christ and understand God's insistence that *'every* tongue should confess that Jesus Christ is Lord'.

RESPONSIBILITIES

Church and Society

🔲🔲🔲🔲

CHRISTIANS HAVE SOMETIMES had a negative view of political life.[1] The third-century theologian, Origen, saw the Roman state as necessary to restrain the disorder of a fallen world but he unflatteringly compared those who were active in political life to a chain-gang of criminals engaged in useful work (*Contra Celsum* IV, para. 70). This judgement may have been coloured, of course, by the virtual exclusion of Christians from public life: more positive estimates followed the establishment of the Christian empire in the fourth century. In all ages, however, there have been Christians so cynical about the futility of politics and with so little hope that state power could be conducive to the justice, peace and love which come from God alone that they have detached themselves from political life while acquiescing in government as a necessary evil in a fallen world.

At the other extreme, there was an attempt from the tenth century onwards, on the part of the ecclesiastical hierarchy of the Western Catholic Church, to assume a tutorial role *vis-à-vis* the state and to enlist lay rulers in an effort to Christianize society. England, which possessed a powerful centralized monarchy from a relatively early date, was not especially fertile soil for this experiment and, long before the Reformation, popes and archbishops were rather less than tutors to English kings and more their tools.

The Reformation of the 1530s marked another stage in the eclipse of the clerical leadership of the English Church. Their economic strength and their influence in the highest councils of state were diminished but, although there was a redistribution of power in the government of the Church, with the Crown and the laity having a greater share at every level in the Church's life, there was no intention to

[1] Open lecture at Kent University, 20 February 1981

reduce the dominant role of the Christian religion in the life of England. On the contrary, Church and Crown were more firmly wedded than ever and strenuous efforts were made to make the life of the people more profoundly and explicitly Christian by education and by the provision of a liturgy in English which demanded the participation of all in the recapitulation of the fundamental texts and affirmations of the Christian faith: the Lord's Prayer, Creeds, Psalms and Commandments. The vision conjured up by the general rubrics for Morning and Evening Prayer in the Book of Common Prayer is of the entire population engaged in a common worship from which would flow common belief and a deeper Christian practice. Use of the common English liturgy, like church attendance, was required by law. It was an experiment which echoed Dante's perception that the Church in its ecclesiastical aspect has authority but should have no power or else it would become corrupt and the secular power has power but, unless it uses its power in the service of the authority of Christ, then it has no justification or validity.

There was no state neutrality in the matter. Law and government action were employed to make England an incubator for simple Catholic faith. Doubtless there were calculations of *realpolitik* involved. England in the previous century had been embroiled in ruinous civil wars which continued to erupt sporadically in the sixteenth century. Common worship and common faith were seen to be a guarantor of national unity. But also from the standpoint of the Church, whose service of God is primary and the spring of all other thought and action, the alliance could appear reasonably and spiritually profitable. Of course, there was and is the ever-present danger that the Church would be seduced from its primary allegiance to pursue reasons of state, comfort, dignity and security, far from the mind of Christ himself; but there are temptations, too, in holding aloof or being hostile to political life and to those who are responsible for the government of society. The Anglican experiment was sustained by the belief that politics and involvement in government were more than a regrettable necessity best left to sinners, but really a way for men formed by the common worship of the Church to forward the creation of a society which would be an incubator of Christianity; a society which would establish a freedom from want and fear, a respect for justice and a framework of Christian observance and morality which would enable citizens to know and finally to respond to the love of God.

It is true that this vision has frequently been obscured by the self-indulgence of a portly Anglican establishment and that the Church of England has needed the criticism of the nonconformist Churches to disturb its slumbers. I believe, however, that the Christian seriousness brought to government by an establishment in which laity as well as clergy have always held positions of responsible leadership, has contributed greatly to the growth of a corporate sense of obligation towards the needy and a respect for justice which has softened social conflict and enhanced the life of every citizen. It is, of course, easy to detail what still needs to be corrected and where welfare provision is not sufficiently generous, or not applied with enough compassion, but it would be foolish to let proper indignation blind us to the achievements of our society in recent centuries or cause us to forget what a rare and fleeting experience in the history of the world it is to live in a society which is secure, reasonably just and moderately prosperous.

What of the other strand of the vision which was designed to make England an incubator of Christianity, namely the formation of a public framework of Christian morality and observance? Education was as vital an element as common worship in sustaining this strategy, particularly since, for various motives, the Church of England put an accent on reason and argument in dealing with its opponents, rather than employing the more vigorous police action favoured by some continental Churches. Rather than found chantries or subscribe to religious houses, my predecessors as archbishops of Canterbury in the sixteenth century were busy founding schools, many of which still exist, and endowing new colleges at the universities. The Church of England still devotes a large proportion of its resources, particularly manpower, to education. There are Church of England chaplains in the universities and polytechnics; and there are Church of England teacher-training colleges. There are large numbers of chaplains in secondary education; and, particularly at the primary level, hundreds of church schools survive as evidence of the extraordinary efforts made by the National Society, the Church of England's main educational agency in the nineteenth century, to provide elementary education for the rapidly increasing population.

Education and common required worship were the means by which the framework of Christian observance and morality was to be constructed and the English Church and state were to be the partners in this enterprise. The vision, of course, was never fully realized. With mixed consequences, numerous faithful Christians were excluded from or abandoned the established Church; and the state, particularly in the last century, had to distance itself from the claims of the Church of England in the interests of social harmony and to avoid excluding talented and industrious non-conformists and Roman Catholics from making a fuller contribution to English life. The Covenanting proposals at present before the Church are perhaps one way of recognizing the impoverishment which came to the English Church with the secession of so many able and sincere Christians and are an attempt to bring healing and to be faithful to the original vision of the Henrician reformers. I am in two minds about whether splinter groups and sects are entirely regrettable, or whether they are a sign of religious vitality. When the state Church did have a unique monopoly, as it did in the state Churches of Scandinavia, its life also manifested a unique torpor.

More recently, there has developed a widespread hostility to the notion that it is proper to use state authority to commend one world-view rather than another. 'Everyone has a right to their own opinion.' This must be one of the most powerful argument-clinching phrases in the language. It is also, of course, true that the population of this country is now more heterogeneous than ever before; there are, for example, many more Muslims than Methodists in contemporary England.

Yet some elements of the vision remain. The Crown, which makes an incalculable contribution to the unity of the country, is still, and even more visibly by television, wedded to the Church of England in birth, marriage, at coronation time and at death. Bishops are still appointed by the Crown and still sit in Parliament, each of whose sessions opens with prayer; and, under the provisions of the 1944 Education Act, Christian worship is still obligatory in state schools. It is notorious, of course, that this provision of the Act is widely ignored, but it is still on the statute book. Since 1944, however, it is undeniable that the neutrality of the state, its disinclination, in an England which harbours a diversity of cultures, to commend one world-view rather than another, has become its dominant posture. This is mirrored by the idea of a 'value-free education', which inspires many teachers. The responsibility for religious education is not invariably given to believers; so-called value-free education often amounts to the propagation of a corrosive scepticism, a reduction of religious faith to the phenomenology of different cults.

We have not made up our minds, however, whether or not to dissolve the Church/state partnership entirely and to admit that England has ceased to have a fundamentally Christian, homogeneous culture or purpose and has become a geographical expression. I would not wish to hurry people into a decision one way or another: a neutral state or a Christian establishment. There is sense in our suspicion of the doctrinaire: the attempt to impose a theoretical pattern on a confusing and diverse jigsaw of ancient institutions and modern attitudes. But, in a situation where we are confronted with choices and decisions and poised between the world of the Christian incubator and that of the neutral state, it would help us to be clearer about the issues involved. Some Anglicans, particularly clergy, manifest a sense of guilt at having a privileged place in society, in government and in education. They believe that Christianity is incompatible with intimacy with the rich and the powerful. They earnestly desire disestablishment and are perhaps its most fervent contemporary supporters. I have much sympathy with their view, but I believe that those who hold that the Christian witness of a Church which is untrammelled but also unsupported by a state connection will be more effective in society as a whole, must be prepared to see the state becoming more rigorously neutral in its attitude to competing world-views.

At present, the state is still not neutral and I want to look at one or two examples of currently controversial questions in order to help plot exactly where we are on the line which runs from confessional to neutral state. Consider the law relating to suicide. Suicide as a criminal offence was removed from the statute book some time ago, but it is still illegal to assist or encourage people to take their own lives. In the Christian tradition, it is absolutely impermissible for the believer to commit suicide; he is usurping the prerogative of God himself. For those, however, who do not believe in God as the author of life and for whom life has become a burden to themselves and to others, why should they not have the right to decide to end it and why should they not be assisted to do this in as painless a manner as possible? Doubtless there would have to be certain safeguards to prevent undue pressure being brought to bear on individuals to take this decision, but on what grounds should the law, as distinct from the law of the Church, discourage suicide as such? Clearly, the state would have a right to legislate on moral matters if the order of society was involved and this presumably is the justification for the recent extension of censorship, which I wholeheartedly support, to forbid statements liable to incite racial hatred. Presumably, however, this sort of consideration would not extend to any change in the law on suicide. Practical considerations aimed at keeping the peace would be the neutral state's chief justification for its actions, but do we really want to surrender all idea that the state should help build a social context for citizens which would be positively conducive to virtue and even to the vision of God?

My second example is blasphemy. The Church, for itself, should never seek to condemn blasphemy. The Church began with Jesus hanging on the cross. They wagged their heads at him and derided him. Purely Christian religious logic would prevent any pressure to make blasphemy an offence against state law. The neutral state, presumably, in the present circumstances would also have little interest in condemning blasphemy since the thought of Mrs White-house leading armies of clergy, foaming at the mouth, to sack Parliament is an unlikely one. The justification for the blasphemy laws is that the state uses its power to produce a context favourable to Christian belief and that the mass of citizens are more disposed to believe that faith is plausible if society discourages belittling or denigration of the chief symbols and concepts of that faith.

We ought to know what we are saying when we disclaim any wish to share further in the partnership between the Church of England and the state which has profoundly marked English society for more than a thousand years. I suspect that the divorce will be carried through, but I do not say this with any self-destructive, pseudo-apocalyptic excitement, but with a determination to make the best of present opportunities without lamenting the past or despairing for the future. We have means to hand for strengthening establishment Christianity in the Covenant and in a more robust and positive attitude to the rights enshrined in the 1944 Education Act. The Church has proved itself able to live with any variety of political systems, but before we welcome with any enthusiasm a future under a neutral state we ought to ask what life will be like in such a fragmented England. Some of those who sing the virtues of pluralism and wish to escape from their close connection with the men of responsibility are demonstrating a clerical variant on the Hebridean croft syndrome, the flight from political responsibility which is so marked a feature of much of the rest of our culture.

It would, of course, be thoroughly small-minded to review relations between the Church of England and English society in terms only of the relations between Church and state. The Church's visible partnership with the Crown and the political system at so many levels still plays its part in reinforcing the desire of the overwhelming majority of citizens to call themselves Christian and to have their children receive a Christian education. How close the popular understanding of Christianity is to the faith of the apostles is another question. But the credibility of the Church/state link in narrowly constitutional terms depends on the combined ability of the Christian Churches to make a significant impact on contemporary English culture. There are signs that the Churches are more adept at calling the nation than convincing it.

The statistics of declining allegiance to the Church of England are well known but difficult to interpret. The core of regular worshippers is about a twentieth part of the population. Those who attend about once a month are about a tenth, but nearly six out of ten people still have a Church of England identity disc hung round their necks. Keenites – those who wish to turn the Church into a species of 'Eucharistic MRA', in David Martin's phrase – are quick to judge as vulgar and unspiritual the common religion of the large constituency who claim allegiance but who do not worship regularly. As Archbishop, I certainly do not find the situation satisfactory, but I believe that it is following the way of Jesus Christ not to proceed by condemnation and to see the Spirit sometimes more clearly at work in those who would rarely feel at home in a church than in some of those whose religious practice is more assiduous. When considering national institutions, however, the number of activists involved is not necessarily crucial. Trade union activists number less than a tithe of those who are involved in regular worship, but still the unions play an unquestioned role in the organization of economic and industrial life.

But how precisely does the national Church serve its wider constituency, and how real is the sense of attachment still admitted to by such a large proportion of the population? The Church still provides evocative symbols, perhaps especially in its church buildings. The reproduction on a myriad of postcards and calendars, set in glades and gentle vales, still points to their power to focus a sense of Englishness which has retained its potency when the uniforms of imperial glory are tattered and even ludicrous. As a diocesan bishop, I was necessarily involved in the process of closing churches in order to divert the financial and human resources involved in their upkeep to places of population growth and greater need. I can assure you that if you have ever tried to close a church you have discovered how deep the foundations lie in popular affection and how many people, who have never darkened the church's door, feel themselves to be involved.

Large numbers of people continue to make use of the

Church's ceremonies. The rites which mark the turning-points in life – birth, marriage and death – where the Church still offers venerable and resonant words, help to give dignity and significance to life. There are also the shared experiences of the Carol Service, Harvest Thanksgiving and Remembrance Sunday, all of which are of relatively recent origin, which give us a rare opportunity to celebrate or mourn together and build up a sense of being at home with one another which is one of the preconditions for a sense of community and the possibility of co-operation across the lines of class and sectional interest.

That these symbols and moments are losing some of their power is, I think, undeniable. The English folk, for a variety of sociological and economic reasons, including mobility and the change in the patterns of industry, is disintegrating into an aggregation. With this disintegration, folk-memory fades and the symbols which feed and are nourished by this memory have a more precarious existence. David Jones catches this very well in his long poem, *Anathémata*. Here, 'at the sagging end and chapter's close', he sees the 'rearguard details in their quaint attire, heedless of incongruity, unconscious that the flanks are turned and all connecting files withdrawn or liquidated – that dead symbols litter to the base of the cult-stone, that the stem by the palled stone is thirsty, that the stream is very low. . . The cult-man stands alone in Pellam's land: more precariously than he knows he guards the *signa*.' And for Robert Lowell, church spires, which are still an evocative image for many, are a painful reminder of the world we have lost:

> In this small town where everything
> Is known, I see His vanishing
> Emblems, His white spire and flag-
> Pole, sticking out above the fog,
> Like old white china doorknobs, sad,
> Slight, useless things to calm the mad.

I feel the force of these lines and would depart from the influential school of modern sociology and analysis associated with the name of David Martin and Edward Norman in my estimate of how far the process of disintegration has gone. It probably reveals me as a typical, middle-class, deracinated liberal of the kind that they suggest is leading the Church to destruction, but I am more agnostic than they are about the real strength of folk-religion and its emblems. I remember many instances and incidents which have helped to form this conviction for me – standing round the bonfire on the fifth of November to find that, apart from a garbled version of the National Anthem, the crowd could not find a song to sing in common; watching the numbers at Remembrance services dwindle and getting the impression that recent changes in both Church and society had reduced the phenomenon of occasional conformity to a point where even at Christmas there were few new faces in the congregation. Perhaps this is a London and Home Counties view and undoubtedly the situation is different north, west and east. Church and society as a whole, however, no longer share the same memories as they did when Milton announced that God speaks first to his Englishmen; and the notion of this country having a special place in the providential scheme of things has steadily given ground before the view of the world, natural in a post-imperial period, which sees this country as victim rather than under the hand of providence; a country subject to random international forces beyond its control, or (the paranoid option) to vast international conspiracies.

But part of the difficulty of my situation, as I seek to contribute to the strategic thinking of the Church of England, is the realization that, while there may be a wasteland from the traditional point of view in North London, Church and society in some other parts of the country may be estranged but they are certainly not divorced. What options, then, are open to the Church?

There are three basic models canvassed: (1) the Episcopal Sect with a parish communion heart: (2) the Church Without Walls, open to the Spirit at work in contemporary society, participating particularly in the struggle for justice and in solidarity with the powerless; (3) a continuation of the National Mission Model, the attempt, so far as possible, to work through the remaining elements of the social order I have tried to sketch, in order to commend the Christian faith.

1 To some extent, the parish communion movement and the liturgical changes of the last two decades have marked a significant shift in the Church of England towards the first strategy. Much has been achieved in improving the morale of the core group and in building up centres of community as the sense of community derived from sharing one national culture decays. I would not wish to deride any of these achievements, but the Parish Communion Model can become rather introverted, the worship of the warmth rising from proximate human bodies and, apart from exceptional cases I know, it has been chiefly successful in a rather narrow, middle-class social stratum. As a sole strategy for the Church of England, it would have us as one Christian group among many others, as David Martin puts it 'warily monitoring the world, making forays at the weak points into the psychic and social structure of the environment'. One of the points at which the Episcopal Sect strategy has encountered resistance is over baptism. There have been laudable attempts to alert parents to the serious implications of baptismal vows; but there has sometimes been a tendency to identify as total indifference to the claims of our Lord what is simply an inability, particularly on the part of working-class parents, to see the closely knit group at St Og's parish church as the sum total of the people of God in a given area. In some areas of the country, however, perhaps in the inner cities, a sect-type fervency with clear frontiers and clear demands with the *esprit de corps* which often results, may be the way for the Church to do its work, but I would be sorry to see this strategy universally adopted.

2 What of the second strategy, that of the Church Without Walls, open to the Spirit in contemporary society, particularly in the struggle for justice and in solidarity with the powerless? I have much sympathy with this view as well. It is indispensable that some members of the Church are at work in this way. A man who is warm can never understand one who is cold and if the Church corporately does not have this experience of sharing the life of the powerless then it has no right to repeat the attitudes and to use the language of the liturgy. Why not then sell the

cathedral, go out from the structures of the Church and enter the world incognito to identify God at work there in the thick of the contemporary struggle? Sacred, according to this view, is not to be distinguished from secular in place or activity, except as an unchristian retreat into an asylum, a ghetto, where some choose to live cloistered from the pain of the surrounding world, feasting on High Art, Gregorian Chant, and Cranmerian English.

This is the way for some Christian outriders, particularly in the anonymity and powerlessness of parts of our great cities, but if this were the whole strategy, their initiative would lack a cutting edge and would lack the resources to sustain it and to raise up new generations of outriders. Assimilation of the Christian world-view to contemporary perspectives is a real danger. The distinctiveness of Christ's way of looking and living needs to be reasserted in signs, in a distinctive community life and language. Then, each generation will produce its outriders. I was particularly struck by this phenomenon in the Soviet Union. Many of the most remarkable and charismatic characters, totally opposed to any compromise with the state and to any dealings with the Church, which they believe colludes with the state, were themselves nurtured by the Russian Orthodox Church, which continues to see its paramount task as transmitting, primarily in the liturgy, the distinctive Christian signs and language which retain their converting power and ability in every generation to rear uncompromising Christians.

3   What, then, of the third and most derided strategy, a continuation of the National Mission Model, a Church concerned to work through the remaining elements of the old social order, a Church pervasive in education, with a special connection with the monarchy and a talent for great state liturgical occasions? This Church is organized to point men and women to God by tending the old roots and associations rather than investing its energies in obsolescent programmes devised by clerical bureaucrats.

One of my heroes among the parish clergy was a priest who refused to have an electoral roll which distinguished between the so-called 'committed' and the uncommitted.

He did not neglect to teach the catholic faith, but he baptized all the children presented to him. He loved the resonances of the Book of Common Prayer and observed stillness and stateliness in the celebration of the Sacraments. He had a mortal horror of the exclusiveness of the phrase 'the people of God', and tried so to conduct himself that he was at the very least a friend to all the inhabitants of his parish. He also prepared a lethal homemade wine called 'In Memoriam' from the rose-petals of withered wreaths from the crematorium. In his last message to his parish, just before retirement, he sighed for the day when parish priests would give up their modish obsession with synods and turn to their true business – bee-keeping, cricket and siring Nelsons. I have been rebuked in the past for admiring his style of priesthood and it is true that it sometimes marches with unbearable complacency and that it is a form of Christian ministry which would have nothing to say in many of the parishes of England, but it has had an honourable history and deserves to be cultivated still.

There is a danger, in a time of restlessness, of yielding to the desire to start afresh, to sweep away the painful fragments of a world which is disintegrating around us. Gleeful, apocalyptic strain is evident in much churchy talk about the Church's future in our society, but it is my conviction that, although the steady progress in which the Church of England is becoming more and more an episcopal sect cannot – and perhaps ought not to – be halted, and although the radical outrider is an indispensable type of Christian soldier, it is too early to abandon altogether the vision of the Church of England as a public body, at the service of the whole nation, serving those in the outer court as well as those in the sanctuary; a Church pervasive, guarding the roots and the memories, pointing to eternity in a time of restlessness and distraction.

This man, so late in time, curiously surviving, shows courtesy to the objects when he moves among, handles or puts aside the name-bearing instruments, the tokens, the matrices, the institutes, the ancilia, the fertile ashes – the palladic fore-shadowings: the things come down from heaven together with the kept memorials, the things lifted up and the venerated trinkets.

Christian Education

🖾🖾🖾🖾

IN 1811, AT the very first meeting of the National Society,[1] one of my predecessors, Archbishop Manners Sutton, presided over an unequivocal statement of its aims. They were 'that the National Religion should be made the foundation of National Education and should be the first and chief thing taught to the Poor according to the excellent liturgy and catechism provided by our Church'. Eighteen months later, when the Society's first annual report was published, these aims had been further crystallized as follows:

> The sole object is our being able to communicate to the Poor generally . . . such knowledge and habits as are sufficient to guide them through life in their proper stations, especially to teach them the doctrine of religion according to the principles of the Established Church and to train them in the performance of their religious duties by an early discipline.

I do not recite these texts to you as historical curiosities. Instead, I wish to inquire whether their letter or spirit has any resonances whatever for us as we deliberate how to use the opportunities that the energy and dynamism of the past has afforded in religious education.

I suspect that not many will be found to sympathize with the aims of the manifesto of 1811. Although it is an uncomfortable fact that 'the Poor' are as statistically evident today as they were at the beginning of the nineteenth century, they are no longer perhaps quite as visible in our society, nor are they regarded, save by the wild men and women of Right and Left, as a source of potential revolution. Religion itself is no longer their opiate and religious instruction is not perceived as a feasible or effective instrument of social discipline.

[1] Address to the National Society, 17 March 1982

The most obvious contrast, however, is that 'the National Religion' is no longer envisaged as 'the foundation of National Education', Indeed, most of us would regard the contemporary status of religious education in general and Christian education in particular as a literal inversion of the nineteenth-century model. The mere inclusion of religious education in many of today's curricula seems to require educational justification, while the abandonment of the Christian hegemony in many agreed syllabuses that I have seen clearly represents a significant shift in the relationship between Church and state in Britain. In both senses, we are now living and educating in a world far removed not only from that of the founding fathers of this Society but even from that of the 1944 Education Act – one of the late Lord Butler's most substantial legacies to us. My determination to involve myself in the area of church schools and religious education owes much to Lord Butler's encouragement. On several occasions he urged me to make the improvement in the standards of religious education one of the themes of my period as Archbishop of Canterbury. He also warned me about some of those in the Church who tended to undervalue and underuse the opportunities offered by the existence of church schools and the provisions for religious education made in the 1944 Act. If it is not too pretentious a thing to dedicate an address to someone, I should like to dedicate what I have to say today to Lord Butler.

The contours and features of our contemporary educational world will be familiar enough to an audience like this. They have been succinctly, if inelegantly, summarized by Edwin Cox as 'an educationally open, thematic-centred, child-related, multi-religious and subject-integrating age'. At its heart lies an assumption that religious education should, in its British setting, directly reflect the current relationship between Christianity and culture. We are frequently told that we live in a 'post-Christian' society. The culture in which Christianity is set is said to be essentially secular – characterized by declining belief and practice, theological and ethical uncertainty, the divergence of religion and morality and dominated by an a-religious technocracy.

A second feature of the context in which we do our work is that, even if we are not yet a secular society (and personally I would wish to question the validity of this analysis), we are nonetheless both a multi-belief and a multi-faith society. With Brixton on my doorstep and Toxteth, which I visited recently, very much on my mind, I have no reason to doubt that this is the case. For many of you who work in church schools, especially in the inner city, the presence of substantial numbers of pupils from non-Christian backgrounds or from a different tradition of Christian life and worship from that of the host community presents an educational challenge just as daunting as that which confronted the founders of this Society.

A third emphasis in religious education is perhaps as familiar to you as it is fascinating to me. It is that whole post-war movement in education which, in attaching much greater importance to the centrality of *experience* in the child's learning processes, has thus served to make religious education increasingly child-centred, rather than subject-centred.

A fourth and final element in the background to religious education is what George Steiner has called 'the end of classical literacy' and what I recently described to the House of Commons Select Committee as 'a kind of verbal Ice Age', where finding words to communicate faith is increasingly difficult. We are, I think, undergoing a real crisis amounting to near-breakdown in our symbolic understanding, especially as far as religion is concerned. Here, for many, the perceived connections between language, symbol and experience seem at best tenuous and at worst dissident or non-existent.

Thus the new questions that face educators and the new kind of milieu in which our schools find themselves are utterly different from the conditions which obtained in the early days of the National Society. It is against such a novel backcloth that some leading questions are being asked about our church schools: 'Are we maintaining and running Christian schools or schools for Christians?' and 'Is there such a thing as educating in a Christian manner?' In response to these very important questions, let me share some of my thinking with you.

First, should we be maintaining and running Christian schools or schools for Christians? This latter proposition, which has good intentions behind it, is based on supporting Anglican requests for specifically Church of England schools. It does not compromise with the obligation to provide cogent Christian teaching and it seals its intention to form an Anglican community by specific provisions for religious education and worship, often with close links with the parish church. Schools following this philosophy will lay down criteria in their published admissions policy which make it perfectly clear that, if there is a queue for admissions, children of worshipping Anglican families will be admitted first. The law, of course, does not allow selection on the basis of a child's attendance or non-attendance at church, but this does not exclude parental commitment. Recent attention has been focused on large primary and secondary Church-aided schools in urban areas. They tend to be popular and therefore applications for admissions exceed the available places. The accusation is that by use of subjective means, such as interviews (which the National Society advises against), the process of selection which takes place makes some schools Anglican middle-class ghettos.

The evidence of such research as has been done suggests that there are very few schools indeed that could so be labelled. However, *intentions* must now be laid bare since the 1980 Act compels schools to publish an admissions policy. The National Society advises a policy based on foundation (that is, Anglican) places and non-foundation places, the proportion of each being determined after discussions by staff and governors about the needs of the community and the church in the area.

It is a great pity that some sections of the London or urban-based media have supposed that this denominational-style model is being applied in the generality of Anglican aided schools. It is not so. There are just over 2000 aided primary schools in the country and just over 100 aided secondary schools (that in itself suggests a task for the future and we should aim for a better balance in our provision). The majority of our schools are neighbourhood, or catchment-area, schools. Many are affected by falling rolls; few have the luxury of choosing from a queue at the door; some are threatened with closure as they very properly co-operate with local education authorities in reducing available places in their area. There are large numbers of teachers and parish priests struggling in these conditions to ensure that church schools serve the whole community. On my visit to Liverpool, I took the opportunity to be briefed about the controversial St Saviour's Church of England School in Toxteth and its future. The parish priest, who has recently arrived in the area, is helping to organize a parents' association, which should improve communications between families and school authorities. His efforts have met with a good and constructive response from the community and this story can be paralleled in many ways and in many places.

Nevertheless, our critics are right to draw attention to the possible social divisiveness in some areas of a policy by which popular, oversubscribed Church-aided schools could, by means of an unbalanced and denominationally selective admissions policy, create schools exclusively for Anglican children.

These considerations, however, do not lead me to a simple endorsement of the formula 'Christian schools rather than schools for Christians'. The term 'Christian school' is evidently somewhat question-begging, because there is no real agreement as to what constitutes 'a Christian way to educate'. It clearly does not just mean having Christian teachers. All of you, I suspect, have encountered teachers who, with no religious commitment, educate in a way that can be described as Christian – manifesting concern for every individual, for the whole person, demonstrating forgiveness and acceptance and building up a caring community within the school. Equally, many of you know others who are professed Christians who educate in a very different way. Another problem concerns the polarities within our own Christian community. The two ends of the spectrum are perhaps illustrated by what David Perman, in his *Change in the Churches*, has called The Pilgrim Church and The Fortress Church: a school built on the lines of the former would be very different from one built on the lines of the latter. And

Christians who insist that the wrath of God carries equal weight with the love of God will probably see the 'Christian way to educate' in a different light from those who insist that the love of God is his supreme attribute.

I have followed the attempts to give some content to the phrase 'a Christian way to educate' with a mixture of admiration, ambivalence and apprehension.

There must be admiration for all the efforts reflected in many of the agreed syllabuses to make Christian education, in Ninian Smart's phrase, 'transcend the informative', to sensitize it towards its own 'implicit' as well as 'explicit' dimensions and to avoid the kind of crude confessionalism so clearly inappropriate for publicly maintained schools in a multi-belief society. There is also a refreshing realism in the recognition that the apparently increasing pluralism of our society demands a fresh approach on the part of those who educate.

My ambivalence is, I hope, of a constructive kind. It takes three forms. The strongest turns on the tension between the Christian educator's need to identify cultural change in order to respond creatively to it and the wayward facility with which highly questionable terms like 'secular', 'plural' and 'multi-cultural' are bandied about so that what is often little more than the newspeak of a section of the intelligentsia gets erroneously elevated to the level of fact. It is, for example, by no means clear whether an age of religious attrition is indisputably upon us, nor whether the divide between the 'religious' and the 'secular' is any more than the fictional device of the sociologists. The orthodoxy which proposes an irreversible decline in mainstream traditional religion has taken some savage blows in the last decade. The situation both in Poland and in Iran has been indisputably misread by those observers nourished by this questionable thesis. Unfortunately, in many parts of our academic establishment it is still virtually unchallenged.

Similarly, as we look around our society, we see that many instances of so-called pluralism are not in fact pluralistic in their own attitudes. It sometimes seems to be assumed that there is general support for a kind of religious faith in pluralism itself. Here in London, as elsewhere, the various immigrant communities –Sikhs,

Pakistanis, West Indians and Cypriots – represent in their urban enclaves not so much pluralism as powerful illustrations of the perennial union of race, culture and religion. Another species of pluralism is the denominational kind that overshadowed the National Society's early years, yet this kind of pluralism, with several denominational firms competing on a fairly open religious market, has actually declined in our own day.

I am ambivalent, thirdly, about what I can only describe as a new kind of indirect confessionalism that has characterized much recent religious education and especially Christian education. Its exponents favour the expression 'search for meaning', but seem to confuse mankind's search for meaning with that of the individual adolescent. They see the task of religious education as setting pupils off on their own search for meaning, to work out their own religion. Such Western Protestant liberal individualism, it seems to me, not merely restricts the understanding of religion to intellectual beliefs and morality but also runs counter to the understanding of religion within those families, whether, for example, Conservative Evangelical, Muslim, or Orthodox Jew, who see meaning as 'given' within a pattern of revelation and who do not want their children set on an individual search for meaning. I am not saying, of course, that many young people are not actively looking for meaning in their lives. But the function of the Christian educator here is surely to help them see the way in which meaning has been given to men's lives through a central religious tradition, rather than suggesting that they have somehow to recapitulate mankind's own search for meaning.

But if I appear to be ambivalent about the high profile some of our educators seem to give to secularism, pluralism and the quest for meaning, and if I regard them as dangerous *idées fixes*, I am positively apprehensive about the strategic consequences of such assumptions, particularly in church schools where we have a special responsibility to develop exemplary models of religious education.

One of my anxieties is that, in our efforts to make Christian education responsive to changes in society, our response is more to certain fashionable imperatives rather than to obligatory and long-standing educational ones. Such things matter, of course, but today's immediate relevance is usually tomorrow's rapid obsolescence. In any case, as Michael Brown puts it in a recent essay, 'the insistence upon the need for a more open and objective approach to religion in schools should not lead us to overlook the radical implications of the logic of religion itself'. Religious education, he says, is in danger of being 'integrated out of existence by assimilation to moral and social studies'.

Similarly, while recognizing that a truly pluralistic society – if such we are – should not merely tolerate diversity but value and nurture it, I must also express the fear that at times we seem tempted to sacrifice too much of our native Christian tradition on the altar of multi-culturism. Just as, in early Victorian England, Christian education was erroneously cast as the key to social order, so, in the late twentieth century, we must take good care not to regard it as the key to good community relations. If we do, we shall find ourselves trapped in a role as constricted and politicized, if not as overtly confessional, as that enunciated in 1811. To be frank, when I read, in one approved syllabus, of the need in religious education 'to set Christianity alongside other religions', as if it were part of some credal smörgåsbord, or that 'it should be part of an education for life in this country that children come to know something of the traditional religion of the land, namely Christianity' (as if Christianity was, like Shakespeare, parliamentary democracy or roast beef, part of a living heritage rather than a living faith), I wonder whether we are not, as Christian educators, selling Christianity short by carrying our anti-confessionalism too far? It sounds uncomfortably like Gibbon's picture of religion in the Roman Empire, in which the various modes of worship which prevailed 'were all considered by the people as equally true, by the philosopher as equally false and by the magistrate as equally useful'.

What role, therefore, do I see for Christian education in the 1980s and beyond? Certainly not as merely part of a minimum body of knowledge designed to present children with what one religious education textbook of my acquaintance rather chillingly calls 'the appropriate forms of reverence'. Nor do I see such education simply as part of our contemporary cultural furniture, to be scrutinized more closely and at greater length than other, non-competing faiths. For, of the organized faiths represented in our culture, Christianity still holds the allegiance of the majority of people, while other faiths are held by quite small groups distributed somewhat unevenly throughout the country. Hence Christianity should be the main perspective studied by most pupils, the living tradition of the host community. Put differently, I think all children, of whatever cultural background, need to understand Christianity, its nature and spirit, its truth claims and its pervasive influence on their present and our past. In this sense, as Professor David Martin has put it, Christian education 'delves deep into the continuities in the human story and it also delves into our own story, our myths of ourselves, part gloss, part hope, part reality'.

But Christianity and Christian education equally address the present, not as a body of teaching expressed, like arithmetic, in difficult concepts, but pre-eminently as a community, a tradition and a way of life, touching the whole of experience and uniquely equipped to answer questions of ultimate concern. It is worth pointing out, perhaps, that, although the increasing divorce of personal morality from personal belief is often held to be a conspicuous feature of the secular city (and one widely reflected in our agreed syllabuses), the hard evidence points in an opposite direction. For many Britons, especially the young, seem to perceive and experience the Christian faith primarily in terms of its moral imperatives and as a prescription for personal conduct. In this sense, in Iris Murdoch's phrase, 'a man's morality is not only his choices but his vision'.

Critics of Christian endeavour in education point to bogies such as indoctrination, ideological pressure and so on as being characteristic of the Christian approach in aiding growing-up. Recently, however, it has become increasingly obvious that political models for teaching are far more likely to close children's options than Christian models. An obvious example is the mushy liberal attitude to sex education. Too light-hearted an attitude to early sexual experience, under the guise of 'freedom', in fact closes young people's options at a time when their identities are far from set. What seems to some a pressure upon children for sexual abstinence, namely a proper concern in teaching religious faith and the Christian tradition, in particular, for a mature attitude to asceticism, in fact keeps children's options open until choice becomes a maturer reality in adulthood. Worship and religious discussion are important and supportive: the real danger is that they become the sole repositories in schools of the Christian dimension.

Of course, we must accept that in classroom teaching the attempt to secure commitment is out of place. No serious treatment of the religious tradition, however, could fail to make it clear that sooner or later commitment is involved. But during the sensitive and difficult stage of adolescence, what we need to ensure is that the young are given the resources for making a decision, rather than required to make it prematurely. There is a passage in the writings of Professor H. H. Price which contains a great deal of wisdom on this matter. It occurs towards the end of his monumental Gifford Lectures on Belief. He is talking about doctrinal practices:

> One of the most important of them is the practice of meditating on certain narratives which we have heard or read, or which have been conveyed to us in other ways, for example by means of pictures or statuary. In Christian theism they are chiefly narrated in the Gospels . . . The important thing is not that we should believe these narratives, or how firmly we believe them, if we do. What is recommended is that we should think of them assiduously and attentively, 'think over' them and ruminate upon them. It is the *entertaining* of these propositions, repeatedly and attentively, which matters at this stage, not the assent to them.

These matters are all highly debatable and I am very glad that the National Society, in collaboration with the Board of Education, is stimulating this debate and I particularly welcome their intention to produce a document which will treat these issues in depth. I am concerned at present, however, to support your work in building Christian schools that will shake the dull, ineffective consensus which pervades so much of our educational thought and practice.

The real justification for the continued existence of church schools must be that they stand for a vision and a protest which are currently undervalued. David Martin puts this point very vividly: 'The secular limits have to be extended both towards the grandeur and the misery of man. Religious education is a refusal to accept the reduction of the world to everyday rationality. It is education because it draws out potentialities overlaid by the reduced one-dimensional consciousness inculcated by the promoters of everydayishness. The religious educator subverts the mundane in favour of the visionary.' There is of course no general recipe for achieving this revolution and the strategy of subversion has to be couched in local terms. This means putting a heavy emphasis on non-Christian religious texts and art in areas where other ethnic cultures are well established.

But in addition to the visionary element, I hope that church schools in their presentation of religious education will also sound the note of protest. It would be a tragedy if their actual justification became that they did no more than beat the world at its own competitive games with an uncritical endorsement of the view that life was a race to the top punctuated by alphas and sporting trophies. There should be no compromise on standards of academic and sporting excellence, but a church school needs to be an explicit protest against any view of education and achievement which puts the accent on success in financial and status terms.

Christianity is also subversive of any form of exclusive national pride or class pretension and puts forward the ideal of a universal brotherhood of those animated by faith, grace and hope. Church schools should also reflect this protest and be on their guard against turning into ghettos of class or racial privilege.

Church schools should be the vehicles for a vision and a protest derived from one of the most dangerously under-estimated forces at work in the world shaping the future – religious conviction. Any educational system which lacked this ingredient would simply be the reflection and the prisoner of a few decades in the history of West European man. We dare not neglect the transforming power of religious conviction – forever renewed even as it is forever denied. It is a source of energy for the transformation we so urgently need in our country. It is by this high standard that church schools ought to be justified and judged.

The Right to Citizenship

🔲🔲🔲🔲

CLERGY MAY OFTEN be ill advised to comment on some of the complexities of current economic and political life;[1] but they are widely deployed in every locality of this country, and not least by actual residence and not only work with their people in inner cities. Through our international obligations we are not ill placed to reflect some of the reactions elsewhere to the image presented by a Nationality Bill. Above all, we deserve a hearing on questions which affect people's fundamental sense of security and the construction of healthy human relationships in our society.

Let me first say that I accept that a new Nationality Bill is needed. In the thirty years since the present Nationality Act was passed, we have seen enormous changes in the relationships between the United Kingdom and the former Commonwealth and Empire – in effect, a move within one generation from a connection based on the idea of an Empire with a common citizenship to what has become a community of self-governing nations. During that time our country has benefited immeasurably, and continues to benefit, from the presence of people who have settled here from Africa, Asia and the Caribbean. Our economy has benefited, our cultural life has been enriched, even – I should say – our religious perspectives have been widened. The other great change has been our entry into the European Community. We have accepted the advantages of a system of free movement of labour throughout the Community, as well as the exposure to continental concepts of citizenship and nationhood.

All these point to the need to reassess our law on citizenship and nationality. I speak of reassessing advisedly.

---

[1] Speech in the House of Lords on the Second Reading of the British Nationality Bill, 22 June 1981

We cannot start with a clean sheet, as though all our past and its obligations could be wiped off. Nor can we make the law depend on the application of a single principle, applied consistently. There are, in fact, a number of considerations which should guide us, if we are to produce a law on Nationality which will continue to be serviceable for the next generation and beyond.

It should first make clear, as the Government have stressed on many occasions, *who* belongs, *who* has a real connection with this country. Belonging is a basic human need, and it is one of the tragedies of the world we live in that there are so many people today who are either formally or effectively stateless, without rights in the country they live in.

A Bill should also recognize the fact that nations today are not sealed off from each other. A constant movement of people is today taking place, people seeking education, work and experience of the world. The encouragement to travel is a mark of a free society. Totalitarian societies, from Plato to the present day, all discourage travel. There must therefore be provision for people from other nations to acquire our citizenship, and for our citizens who travel for longer or shorter periods to be assured that they and their children will not be disadvantaged.

Lastly, and above all, it must do justice to the existing fabric of social life and not inject uncertainty where none existed before. This is of particular importance in a society like our own, which is still learning, often painfully, what is required if people of different ethnic origins, cultures and religions are to live together in mutual respect.

How does the present Bill look when measured against these criteria? I pay tribute to the patience of Ministers in listening to criticisms – and indeed going out to meet the critics – and to their willingness to make changes in the Bill. I hope that will continue for I am bound to say that in terms of the considerations I have mentioned, the Bill is still seriously defective. The message that I am receiving from churches, particularly in areas where there are large numbers of people who originally derived from the African, Asian and West Indian countries of the Commonwealth, is that this Bill is causing very real anxiety, and even fear, among this section of our population. It is a fact that the great majority of those who have settled in the United Kingdom from these countries during the last thirty years regard themselves as British and have totally identified themselves with this country. Their children, who are now becoming adults, were mostly born here and have known no other country. They passionately want to be accepted by the rest of the population as the full British citizens which they believe themselves to be.

There will be no doubt in the new categories where British citizens will belong. They will have the right of abode, the right to enter without let or hindrance. They will form the largest group out of the five – and it so happens that almost all of them, over 96 per cent, will be white people. The British people in the four other groups will almost all be of non-European descent. This main scheme remains untouched by the amendments that have been made to the Bill in another place.

So the anxiety which this Bill has produced arises because it seems to many to raise question marks where these did not exist before. First, the Bill is so complex that it is difficult for most people to understand. That is not good in a matter which affects such basic rights as citizenship. Second, it requires many people to register where there is no such requirement now. This will in itself be an enormous initial burden on those who will have to administer the Act and will lead to delays and uncertainties. Third, those concerned fear that it may be difficult and certainly time-consuming to produce and to prove the evidence which this process will require, to say nothing of the cost involved. For the simple possession of a British birth certificate or a British passport will no longer be a guarantee of British citizenship.

Can the anxieties of so many of my inquirers be allayed, for example the man who writes: 'I find it nightmarish to imagine that in eight years' time a child taken to hospital or wanting to go on a school trip or entering some other situation wanting a passport, might be subjected to inquiries about his or her right to be here'? This is what I am hearing from clergy from many parts of England who have no political axe to grind in this particular matter.

Uncertainty about one's position leads very easily to a feeling of being unwanted, and that is serious. Let me quote from a bishop who works in East London:

> Hardly a week goes by without my facing some father or member of a family who, divided by thousands of miles, experiences the acute anxiety of potential or permanent separation from their nearest and dearest. Whilst we all recognize that there must be clarification of the Nationality issues, ethnic minority communities in the East End certainly feel this is a major intrusion into their peace of mind and their proper membership of our community. So little will be achieved because the effect on immigration will be minimal and the cost will be so great in terms of a sense of rejection and vulnerability.

A clergyman working in South London writes:

> The time limit on the right to registration is the cause of great distress. Although it has been extended to five years people feel the pressure of having to make a choice and carry it through within a specified time, especially where it means forgoing another citizenship.

Recently the Home Secretary kindly invited me to bring seven clergy from Brixton to talk about the recent troubles in that area. The people who came were all deeply involved in the community life of Brixton and want to help in finding answers to the problems there. They were positive and constructive, and the Home Secretary listened most attentively to them. Much of the discussion was naturally about policing and about such contributory factors as unemployment and housing, but they went on to say that this Bill has contributed to the increased tensions because of the insecurity and the feeling of being unwanted which it has generated. The proposals in this Bill have to be seen in the context of all the other experiences the ethnic minorities have been through. It is not an Act to be passed in a vacuum.

I recognize that there are evil forces from the Left and the Right ready to play on people's fears and to stir up divisions, but we must not present them with any material with which to do so. What is needed above all from a new British Nationality Act is reassurance, reassurance that could only have been provided by a measure whose basis was seen to be equality of respect and regard. It would not have been impossible, not even difficult, to frame such a measure. It would surely have been no more difficult to frame than this amazingly complicated Bill before us.

The sort of Bill we needed was primarily one which first of all maintained the principle of automatic citizenship at birth for any person born on the territory of the United Kingdom. I do not find convincing the reasons which have been advanced by the Government for abandoning this principle. Its abandonment has been one of the main causes of anxiety among the ethnic minorities. Many of them have jumped to the conclusion that it is a prelude to repatriation. Of course there is no justification in the Bill itself for this fear. But people who have already been afraid for years of repatriation are bound to be alarmed by such a proposal. The new uncertainties about citizenship of children born here after the Act are going to be no good to us individually and no good to us as a community. What shall we gain? A few thousand people a year, born in the United Kingdom, will not get our citizenship. Many more thousands will be uncertain, or unable to prove, whether they have citizenship or not. Civil Servants will have far more work than now as a result. And advice agencies and all those whose work is pastoral or connected with social welfare will be bombarded with worried inquiries from parents. What great benefit – indeed what small benefit – is it supposed to bring this country that the number of people who are its citizens will be diminished annually by some tiny amount proportionate to the whole?

I have already mentioned this question of registration. Is it surprising that there should be bitterness when, having lived here for perhaps twenty-five years, and having come here as British from birth – which is true of many West Indians who came here when their countries were still colonies – people should have to fill in a form and pay £50 in order to be British all over again? Could not a simpler system have been devised – and one which left no doubt about the maintenance of existing rights and entitlements? Take, as an example, what appears to be inexcusable meanness in respect of one group of people, namely those non-patrial Commonwealth citizens who settled here before the commencement of the 1971 Immigration Act. They came here entitled to registration as British citizens after five years' ordinary residence; that automatic entitlement was preserved by the 1971 Act. Now it is to be ended if it is not exercised within five years after the present Bill becomes law.

The guiding principles of a new Bill should surely have been to reassure rather than to alarm, to ensure that no child is born here stateless or born abroad to a British parent stateless, and to reaffirm the existing rights of those living and legally settled here. If these simple requirements were met by the Bill, the fears that have been aroused – some of them needlessly and mistakenly – should be allayed and a redefinition of our nationality would become a source of new self-confidence for all our people. There should be a security about British citizenship. There should be a clear message about the sort of society which we have become. I have spoken in general terms, but there will be many others to look more specifically at the Bill. I am concerned about impressions and about reassurance.

When the legislation of any country defines what its nationality is to signify, and who is to hold it, it establishes more than a set of regulations which particular individuals have to satisfy. It says how it conceives the nation. For example, the citizenship law of the German Federal Republic, West Germany, provides that the inhabitants of the German Democratic Republic are citizens of the Federal Republic. An East German arriving in West Germany is therefore already a citizen. He needs no immigration papers. He has no need to go through naturalization. That is not only convenient for East Germans, it says something about how the West Germans conceive of the German nation. The rules for the nationality of non-Germans are very restricted.

By contrast, Canada gives preference within its overall immigration restrictions to people of no matter what national or ethnic origin who speak French or English, and makes it comparatively easy for them, once accepted for entry, to become full citizens. In this way many French-speaking Lebanese, for example, have been accepted for settlement with a view to their becoming citizens.

The present Bill, even though it has no preamble declaring a theory of national identity, cannot avoid establishing by its provisions themselves a picture of British national identity. The fact is that many feel that it gives a picture of first- and second-class citizens. It is no help to an individual Jamaican or Barbadian to say to him: 'Don't worry about this Bill, because you have been registered here and your children were born here so you will be all right.' Or: 'You still have five years in which you can register as a British citizen and get full rights here.' The Bill does not seem to spell out the securities of citizenship within a multi-racial society that this country has now become.

I began by asking for a hearing from church opinion. I conclude by reminding you that one of the greatest of my predecessors as Archbishop of Canterbury was Theodore of Tarsus. He would have had some difficulty in establishing his citizenship under the present Bill. However, in the seventh century he unified the English Church and it is no exaggeration to say that he gave a shape not only to the Church but to a nation over against its separate kingdoms.

It is because this Bill will give a shape and character to our future society that it is of such importance for us all. Though a Bill is needed, it may even be questioned whether this is the right moment to bring it in. It is at least my hope that this House will take its opportunity as a revising chamber to remove some of those aspects of the Bill which have caused the deep concern that I have tried to voice.

Race Relations: The Way Forward

🔲🔲🔲🔲

MANY HOPEFUL INITIATIVES in the field of community relations have been launched in Birmingham,[1] and you have continued to be energetic pioneers when so many others have become weary and dispirited. The reasons for this depression about current attitudes and the future pattern of relations between the communities in the new multi-racial Britain are not hard to understand.

Even after Brixton and Toxteth, there is still a frightening lack of awareness about the nature and seriousness of the problem. Even after Lord Scarman's Report there is still a tendency to place all the blame for the disturbances on 'criminal elements'. It would be foolish to deny that there is some truth in this analysis, but in Martin Luther King's words, riot is also 'the voice of the unheard'. I am not suggesting that such attitudes are likely to be found in this hall, but as I travel around the country I still frequently meet suburban-dwelling decision-makers who claim that there is no racial problem in their leafy avenues, when their own lack of urgency and lack of conviction that measures have to be taken to redress racial disadvantage is itself a major contribution to the problem.

Lack of urgency, and inactivity, however, are sometimes less frightening than simplistic prescriptions, whether hostile or well-meaning. It is the daily experience of most people here that when you examine the community patterns of a particular locality the 'racial problem' dissolves into a bewildering welter of cross-currents and sub-plots. Asian and West Indian populations are as different from one another as they are from the indigenous Anglo-Saxons. There are not only tensions between minority groups, but also within families there are often acute differences of attitude, and conflicts between the genera-

---

[1] Address to the Birmingham Community Relations Council, 2 July 1982

tions. In particular, there is a sub-culture of disadvantaged young West Indians who do not participate in society as we understand it at all. Then, while I do not generally subscribe to conspiracy theories to explain events, it would be naïve to refuse to accept the evidence that the brew is being stirred by extremist groups at both ends of the political spectrum. I am glad to be able to say that in Birmingham your Chief Constable led the way for many other parts of the country in successfully applying to the Home Secretary to ban marches by extremist groups bent on winding up racial tension.

The complexity and difficulty of the problems have immobilized some, while others have been wearied by the impotence of so much talk about racial attitudes and problems, and bored to the point of exhaustion by the soporific clouds of platitude generated by the virtuous and detached. An archbishop is particularly exposed to this danger since he can rapidly develop what one critic described as the 'fatal facility of continuous utterance'.

There is abundant pessimism about the possibility of our society remaining coherent and united in the future, much of which is justified, but it is also true that defeatism ensures defeat. Complacency is inexcusable, but we can be encouraged by what has already been achieved and the way in which attitudes have been changed, particularly in the aftermath of last year's riots. Much of the credit for this must go to Lord Scarman and his Report.

I have heard some of those, clergy and others, who have had long experience of work in the inner city, claim that Lord Scarman has said nothing new and that those in touch with the situation had been predicting trouble for years but nobody listened. That may be true, but the way in which Lord Scarman presented his findings, tracing the course of events, and examining police tactics in language of extraordinary purity and precision, has given his Report an unassailable moral authority which has compelled attention and respect from those not disposed to listen to the previous warnings and criticisms.

In particular, the Scarman Report has stimulated a positive response from police authorities. In the beautiful clarity of the study it is easy to be critical of the way in which the police do their dangerous work, but on the streets, faced directly with threats and abuse and sometimes violence, it is not so easy to preserve a philosophic attitude. Young blacks and young police officers have much in common. Both are minority groups under pressure, wary of any threat from the other. It is understandable that both groups in times of stress should retreat behind tribal stockades of prejudice and bigotry.

This question of relations between the police and the ethnic communities is obviously of crucial importance if Britain is to be a coherent and peaceful entity, with all the racial elements which now make up our country contributing and going forward together.

It is to the credit of many leading policemen that they have not retreated into defensive positions. In particular, I have been heartened by a recent lecture by Sir Kenneth Newman who is to become the Metropolitan Police Commissioner in October. After emphasizing that there are 'thousands of young black people living in sensitive areas in London who are basically law-abiding and who are by no means alienated from white society', he goes on to sketch a new strategy for the police. He contrasts pro-active with reactive policing and favours the former policy in which the police take the initiative in acting on the environment rather than merely responding to it. He is among those who believe that the police should try to do more in preventing crime by greater contact and co-operation with the public and other social agencies in the locality.

Sir Kenneth's lecture also states that in our society visible accountability is one of the conditions for effective policing. At the same time he endorses a point made by Lord Scarman that new forms of consultation should be worked out to ensure that the police, their policies and operations are in touch with, and responsive to, the communities they police. As many police officers recognize, a policing style has to be negotiated with the local community to provide the basis for the greatest possible co-operation in the vitally important matter of maintaining social order and respect for the law. Violence ought not to be condoned. The police have the responsibility for combating crime and protecting society from those who commit crimes. This cannot be done effectively without the co-operation of the community in general. Part of Sir Kenneth's prescription for achieving this co-operation is that the police should, especially in multi-racial inner city areas, reduce to a minimum abrasive street encounters while focusing their efforts on the selective targeting of the people actually committing the street robberies.

Sir Kenneth is by no means a lone voice in this vitally important area which is crucial for future racial harmony in this country. Sir David McNee, the present Metropolitan Police Commissioner, has also said in a recent statement that 'the best defence against a repeat of last year's public disorder is not riot squads and water cannon, but public opinion and officers who get alongside the communities'.

I know that in Birmingham some important pioneer work has been done, particularly in the Handsworth area, to explore the practical implications of this community policing strategy. Your experience will be increasingly valuable as more and more areas of the country recognize that a new approach is necessary. Lord Scarman's Report and the ensuing debate has contributed powerfully to this change of attitudes, and I hope that as the immediate shock of the events of last summer recedes we shall not sink back into indolence and complacency. The consequences of doing nothing will be dire. As the Red Queen in *Alice* said, 'to stand still is to go backwards'.

I hope Lord Scarman's Report will not be consigned to the library shelves like so many documents before it. There is a sobering comment at the end of the report of the Kerner commission, set up by President Johnson after the 1967 disturbances in the United States. The black scholar, Dr Kenneth Clarke, referred to the great legion of good but forgotten reports. 'I read the report of the 1919 riot in Chicago, and it is as if I were reading the report of the investigating committee on the Harlem riot of 1935, the report of the investigating committee on the Harlem riot of 1943, the report of the McCone Commission on the Watts riot. I must again in candour say to you it is a kind of Alice in Wonderland, with the same moving picture shown over and over again, the same analysis, the same recommendations, and the same inaction.'

Relations between the police and the ethnic communities are of course only a small, albeit important, part of the picture of race relations in this country, but it is an area where I believe there has been modest movement and modest progress which should nerve us with the conviction that there is a way forward. Britain is inescapably a multi-racial country. Any talk of repatriating people who have sometimes lived here for more than two generations or who are no longer welcome in their countries of origin is a dangerous fantasy. We are, in fact, a multi-racial society, and the choice we have is between working to make this fact a matter for pride and celebration, or drifting into a situation where this fact is a matter for lament and despair.

Last year's Handsworth Festival gave us all encouragement and a picture of what things would be like. John Brown, the social analyst, who has been working on police and community relations in Handsworth, described the scene like this:

> People of all races moved freely at ease, stopping to watch the entertainments or just to sprawl on the grass to take the sun, while the kids rushed off for lollies and the ice cream van. Brummies in shirt sleeves brushed shoulders with girls in ethnic dresses, Sikh elders with long white beards, young Rastas in sharp gear. And there in the midst of it all an old English couple selecting their spot to sit, spreading a cloth on the grass, laying out their picnic with care, eating in peace: key symbols of personal security: the acid test of it all.

How do we ensure that this foretaste becomes typical? I should like to assemble a general strategy for going forward together under four headings: (1) immediate actions; (2) symbolic gestures; (3) the long-term strategic approach; (4) the visionary element.

Immediate Action

I am referring to things that can be done relatively quickly and cheaply, especially in the vital area of improving communications within the community. I was delighted to see from your annual report that the process of consultation which Sir Kenneth Newman believes to be desirable between ethnic groups and the police already has a history in Birmingham, both at the level of the local community and through the formal meetings of the Police Liaison Committee. This picture does not hold good, however, for every part of the country, nor is it true for every section in society. Even the Christian Churches have lived until recently in watertight compartments, and old-established religious bodies have been content to live in ignorance of the flourishing black-led churches. In Birmingham you have once again taken the lead in building bridges between the various Christian bodies in an unpatronizing way which seeks to harness the strength of all the churches for the service of the whole community. There is no excuse now for members of the Church of England not to know their local cherubim and seraphim.

But not only the churches but every organization in the community – rotary clubs, sports organizations, unions, chambers of commerce, and the rest – ought to have on their agenda the question of improving communications with the various ethnic groups.

This local work is more important, I believe, than any further legislative action. We already have a legal framework to express our repugnance for excessively racialist attitudes, but at the very least we can signal our commitment to finding a way forward to harmonious race relations by refraining from insensitive legislation. In this connection, I still believe what I stated in Parliament at the time, that the Nationality Bill brought little positive gain at the cost of increasing suspicion and insecurity in some of the most sensitive areas of the country. We shall all have a hard struggle to minimize the social consequences of the new Act.

Symbolic Gestures

Our culture is often dismissive of the importance of symbolic gestures. They are brushed aside as mere gestures or 'tokenism'. Now of course some symbolic gestures can be fraudulent or cynical, but appointing black or brown newsreaders or protesting about the continued sale of *Little Black Sambo* are not actions which strike me as trivial or laughable. Very few of us subject every idea or attitude we have to rigorous analysis or intellectual scrutiny. Most of the time we take our tone and our opinions from the prevailing notions around us. Racism is fuelled by a culture which does not permit black or brown people to assume positions of authority, such as reading the news on television or being bishops or judges, and the foundations of such a racist culture can be laid in childhood by books and pictures which never explicitly, but insidiously, communicate a condescending attitude to other races and religions.

One thing which most Englishmen cherish very lovingly is their reputation for having a sense of humour. I belong sufficiently to this tradition to believe that people without a sense of humour tend to lack a sense of proportion and ought not to be trusted. But this saving humour can easily tip over into flippancy and easy talk about things which are deeply offensive if you belong to a minority and which nourish more overt kinds of racial intolerance.

We do derive much of our understanding of the world and our sense of right or wrong relations to it through symbol. People who live in a monarchy where the royal family plays such an important part in exemplifying social and family values and in giving people a sense of belonging, ought not to be blind to the extreme importance of the level of symbolic communication. Yet I was surprised when I decided to invite Mrs Esmé Beswick, a West Indian Pentecostal pastor in Brixton, to take part in the service welcoming the Pope at Canterbury, to be criticized for gimmickry by some very high-minded people, who could not by any stretch of the imagination be accused of racism. I profoundly disagreed. The symbol was not a fraud, but a magnification of the truth that all the races, both in this country and worldwide, must co-operate in building the future together, and are in fact doing so, under the inspiration of the religious vision of the brotherhood of man and the fatherhood of God. I would defend the presence of inter-faith friends at the same service for similar reasons.

Public events and the faces to be seen in positions of authority should be scrutinized to make sure that the symbolic communication they inevitably make is telling the right tale and contributing to national unity.

The Longer-Term Strategy

Better communications and symbolic actions will only be cosmetic measures unless they are accompanied by a longer-term strategy and specific policies to redress the social disadvantages under which some ethnic groups labour. This brings me to the question of what has been called 'positive discrimination'. The phrase is unhelpful because the word 'discrimination' now carries such a heavy charge of unfairness that it damns the policy before it has had a hearing. I prefer the American term 'affirmative action'. It is cumbersome, but some such phrase is needed to alert the whole community to the fact that the ethnic minorities do suffer real disadvantages which prevent them realizing their full potential and which makes special action to overcome them essential. The areas in which 'affirmative action' is particularly needed were pointed out by Lord Scarman in a recent lecture in Westminster Abbey. They are education, job training and job opportunities. This means giving to certain parts of our cities a measure of priority in the allocation of resources.

The decay of the inner city areas is not the result of inexorable natural forces – it is at least partly the result of policies which have encouraged people to move out of the city centres into new housing areas with better facilities. When substantial immigration was taking place in the 1960s the immigrants were not eligible under the local-period-of-residence rules for council housing, so they had to buy or rent in the least expensive areas which were the decaying inner city slums. The result is the black or brown areas of today in which the property is often run down and substandard. In the same areas schools are old and ill equipped, and there is a lack of open space and recreational facilities. The conditions are exacerbated by disproportionately high unemployment and limited job opportunities for black or brown school-leavers.

This is a familiar story, but it is important to tell it again and again. As specific policies and incentives had a part in creating the present situation, so it is just and reasonable that there should be 'affirmative action' to deal with some of the injustices and disadvantages created. At the very least this will include making special education provision for teaching language skills, special job training schemes for inner city areas, and encouragement to employers to provide more job opportunities in those areas. Race is an important factor in being disadvantaged in Britain, and this has contributed to the widespread sense of rejection and alienation which exists among some black and Asian young people. We have not understood the situation if we fail to recognize this and we have no right to talk glibly about reconciliation withour recognizing that social justice is an essential condition for genuine and long-lasting reconciliation.

Much of what I have said has considerable financial implications and involves statutory bodies and governmental agencies, but I do not wish to sound as if I thought the devising and implementing of a long-term strategy for community relations was a matter for Whitehall alone or some other comfortably removed Aunt Sally. Private employers and voluntary organizations also clearly have a responsibility.

I remember being in Liverpool sitting around the table with some of the principal employers of the town and doing some sums about the percentage of coloured people employed in their concerns. Just the simple revelation of how few were employed, in comparison with the percentage of black and brown people in the town, came as a surprise and a shock to many present. I cannot of course say whether this discovery deeply changed any attitudes or whether the extravagance of an expansive moment rapidly faded, but such information needs to be hammered home again and again until it becomes part of the mental furniture of all of us. I understand that you are having a similar exercise here in Birmingham where you are looking at the recruitment policies of some of the departments of the Council.

But it is futile to point the finger at others when one's own house needs to be put in order. I believe that the Churches currently do make a contribution to improving attitudes and building bridges between different sections of the community, but their untapped potential is even greater. I hope you will forgive me if I take most of my examples from the Church I know best, the Church of England, and will understand that I do not by this intend to undervalue the work of any of the other Churches which have so often been an example and an inspiration to us.

The Church begins with considerable advantages. We have substantial buildings in the inner cities – sometimes the only local buildings which can be used for community purposes. Our clergy, unlike many other professional workers, live in the areas they seek to serve and thus have special opportunities to discover the problems and the anxieties of their neighbours. I know from personal experience of Brixton and Lambeth that we have some very able and dedicated men and women working in the inner city who can and do play a crucial part as intermediaries between different parts of the community, while providing neutral ground where mutually hostile groups can meet.

There are, of course, temptations to withdraw from the inner cities. The work is costly and difficult. There is often very little response. In some areas we have had to close churches and to withdraw workers but, as far as I have any influence, I am determined that we should maintain our presence in the most sensitive areas and allocate our resources accordingly. This is the position of many bishops and church leaders, and I was particularly delighted in visiting Liverpool earlier this year to discover that part of the Church's response to the Toxteth troubles was to increase its manpower there.

The Churches can be intermediaries in another sense, too. There are very few institutions which are able to bring together on terms of relative equality those who live in the areas where the ethnic groups are concentrated and those who inhabit the suburbs. Much more needs to be done in this field and I hope that the idea of twinning parishes and institutions from different social and ethnic backgrounds will continue to spread. I have just visited St John's College, Durham, which has developed a relationship with a college in Northampton which trains ministers for a number of black-led Pentecostal churches. Links like these ought to be fostered energetically.

At a national level, too, there are departments and church agencies seeking to foster the kind of local projects in which you are so much involved in Birmingham. I would mention in particular the Community and Race Relations Unit of the British Council of Churches. It was set up in 1971 and is chiefly concerned with producing materials and information to help those involved in the work of education for a multi-racial society.

For me, the most telling picture of the positive contribution that the Churches can make to community building and better race relations was provided by a visit to Notting Hill at Eastertime last year for a Holy Week procession. Free Churches, Roman Catholics and Anglicans had combined to assemble a multi-racial cast for a Cecil B. de Mille-style passion play, involving large forces and a march through some of the streets which were the scene of rioting a few years ago. Christ was a West Indian, partly, as he ingenuously explained to me, because there was an obvious black candidate for the part of Pilate, and symbolically it would have been particularly unfortunate if he had been paired with a white Christ. It was a moving demonstration of what could be done when people of different backgrounds shared a common vision.

The Visionary Element

It is in our interests that racial attitudes should be improved. Order, prosperity and all the amenities of a civilized life will suffer if they are not. But enlightened self-interest is rather a cold and remote god to whom few sacrifices are made, and it is boldness and self-sacrifice that we need if our difficulties are to be overcome. Very few people fall passionately in love with a rational calculation.

Societies, if they are to thrive, and be united, need a story which explains in vivid pictorial form where the members of that society have come from and what they stand for. In sharing such a common story, an aggregation is turned into a community with some direction and purpose. This is precisely what happened to the wanderers who formed the nation of Israel under the impact of the story of the exodus from Egypt.

During its history Britain has been influenced by a number of stories. Some have purchased national cohesion at the cost of asserting Anglo-Saxon superiority. The arrogance of these stories has been found out by history. The sun has set on the British Empire and the imperial story has been overtaken by the march of events. But those old stories also had a nobility about them. We were the island of the free, where tyranny was restrained by equality under the common law and a great range of opinion was tolerated, and eccentrics were cherished, not persecuted. This story was taught in music, words and pictures. It was part of the reason why many of our black and brown citizens wanted to make their future here.

It is no part of equipping ourselves for multi-racial harmony to respect every tradition except our own. The period when our institutions and traditions were scoured and scrubbed by satire was doubtless valuable, but the time has come for 'affirmative action' in this department as well. Our national story was not all romantic cover for exploitation and oppression. There are precious elements in it which could help us to realize that racial prejudice involves letting ourselves down.

That is not enough, however. Tolerance is first cousin to indifference, and the way forward must be through building one another up and cherishing one another's strengths and talents. The religious view of life provides a basis for treating men and women from different cultures as our brothers and sisters, and makes talk of fraternity a reality and not just a pious or sentimental aspiration. Our human brotherhood flows from our dependence on God as his children. I believe that both these concepts have been enlarged by the arrival of Asian, African and Caribbean groups in our cities.

I want to explain that statement carefully, particularly in its implications for inter-faith relations. Religion has, of course, often been one of the sources of division between racial groups. There has been a tendency to set our Christian truth against the possibly diabolical fantasies of the other religions. But while our conviction about the truth of the Christian faith remains, we are now less anxious to pass judgement on the source of the different set of religious convictions of people we have come to know and respect as our neighbours. As a Birmingham professor, John Hick, has said: 'When the response to the new neighbour has been motivated by genuine Christian love, we can say that the old theological problem has been outflanked by a new religious event.'

It is so often new circumstances which reveal the divine Spirit's next word and this is only rarely given to us in the form of new verbal formulation. The presence of the ethnic groups with their different religious traditions has given new breadth and generosity to our vision of the brotherhood of man and the fatherhood of God. Also, in the consequent dialogue between the faiths, the result, in my experience, has been far from a dilution of faith, but rather a fresh grasp of what is particular and precious about Christianity coupled with a growth of knowledge of, and respect for, other religious traditions.

The shift in religious perception was recognized in Birmingham in the early 1970s with the introduction of a multi-faith syllabus for religious education. The storm over the appearance of Mr Marx in this document perhaps concealed what a revolutionary concept it was.

I both cherish our national story, shorn of its imperial pretensions, and believe that this story, now illuminated by the vision of the brotherhood of all races rooted in the universal fatherhood of God, has a power to move men and women to acts of friendship and self-sacrifice in a way that no appeals to enlightened self-interest can.

It will be obvious from what I have said, however, that our problems with the disintegration of our national story and the weakness of our vision of the divine family both antedate and are independent of the arrival of the new ethnic groups. The new arrivals from Asia, Africa and the Caribbean have sometimes been blamed for the incoherence of Britain but, in reality, British society was in the process of being atomized long before they arrived. What coherence there was has decayed under the impact of materialism and assertive sectional and self-interest. Your Community Relations Officer, Mr Chakravarti, introduced his report with a quotation from John Donne: 'No man is an island.' The poet knows this to be the truth, but knows also with tragic intensity that man does not behave as if it were. Despite long traditions of stability in our society, Donne's pessimistic vision stares us in the face:

> 'Tis all in peeces, all cohaerence gone
> All just supply, and all Relation:
> Prince, Subject, Father, Sonne, are things forgot,
> For every man alone thinkes he hath got
> To be a Phoenix, and that then can bee
> None of that kinde, of which he is, but hee.
> This is the world's condition now . . .

It was to a country going down that way that the immigrants came. I am not sanguine but I do have hope that the presence and the fresh insights of the most recent members of our national family will recall us to the best in the English story and help us to see that, with the help of our new members, it has a future in building a vision of world brotherhood. They bring rich gifts, and they have much to offer in building the Britain of the next century. All those of us in this room who are, in our various ways, people of influence have the opportunity and the choice of helping to create conditions in which they can give of their best, or we can persist in attitudes which will almost certainly ensure that they do their worst.

The Falkland Islands

🔲🔲🔲🔲

THE FIRST NOTE in this service[1] is thanksgiving. We began with particular thanksgiving for the courage and endurance of those who fought in the South Atlantic and that is where my sermon starts.

What I have heard about the conduct of the British forces in and around the Falkland Islands has moved and heartened me. I have experienced battle myself and know that it is no mean achievement to preserve the restraint and display the courage shown by so many involved in this conflict. I was particularly impressed by the report of one journalist who admitted that he had started the campaign with a fairly standard stereotyped view of the forces – effete officers leading unreflective men. He was converted by the Falklands experience and returned with a deep respect for those who had fought bravely, without turning into 'automata'. He was moved by the mature way in which grief was openly expressed over the loss of comrades and admired the lack of rancour shown in attitudes towards the enemy. Another eye-witness has described to me the determination shown at every level to achieve objectives with the minimum use of force. At the hard-fought battle of Goose Green the reaction was not the conquerors' triumph, but 'thank God it's stopped'. It is right to be proud of such men.

There is much to give thanks for in all this now that the attempt to settle the future of the Falkland Islanders by armed invasion has been thwarted, but the men who served in this campaign would be the first to say that while we are paying tribute to the armed forces we should not forget the perseverance and courage of those who have been defending the lives and laws of the citizens of this country in Northern Ireland over a number of years.

[1] Sermon at the Falkland Islands Service, St Paul's Cathedral, 26 July 1982

While giving thanks, however, we also mourn for grievous losses. Thank God so many returned, but there are many in this cathedral who mourn the loss of someone they love and our thoughts go out to them. We must not forget: our prayers for remembrance will not end this day. They remind us that we possess the terrifying power for destruction. War has always been detestable, but since 1945 we have lived with the capacity to destroy the whole of humankind. It is impossible to be a Christian and not to long for peace. 'Blessed are the peacemakers for they shall be called the sons of God.' This was one of the themes to which the Pope repeatedly returned during his visit to this country. His speech in Coventry was particularly memorable when he said: 'War should belong to the tragic past, to history. It should find no place on humanity's agenda for the future.'

I do not believe that there would be many people, if any, in this cathedral who would not say amen to that. War is a sign of human failure and everything we say and do in this service must be in that context. The problem is that war belongs to the tragic present as well as to the tragic past. At the beginning of this century, in a noble book, *The Great Illusion*, by Norman Angell, the irrational character of war in a modern world was precisely described. The thesis is that in a world of economic interdependence you cannot injure another state without damaging your own interests. We flourish and become prosperous, not by raiding and pauperizing our neighbours, but by building them up as ever better markets for our manufactures.

Yet war, demonstrably irrational and intolerable, has left a terrible mark on this century. It has claimed tens of millions of victims and even now occupies some of the best talents and resources of the nations. The great nations continue to channel their energies into perfecting weapons of destruction and very little is done to halt the international trade in arms, which contributes so much to the insecurity of the world. In the most heavily armed area, the Middle East, every day seems to bring fresh bad news of man's willingness to resort to the irrational and the intolerable in pursuit of his territorial and ideological ambitions. Angell was writing at the end of a period of relative peace. We cannot be even as sanguine about the human future as he was. Our hope as Christians is not fundamentally in man's naked goodwill and rationality. We believe that he can overcome the deadly selfishness of class or sect or race by discovering himself as a child of the universal God of love. When a man realizes that he is a beloved child of the Creator of all, then he is ready to see his neighbours in the world as brothers and sisters. That is one reason why those who dare to interpret God's will must never claim him as an asset for one nation or group rather than another. War springs from the love and loyalty which should be offered to God being applied to some God-substitute, one of the most dangerous being nationalism.

This is a dangerous world where evil is at work nourishing the mindless brutality which killed and maimed so many in this city last week. Sometimes, with the greatest reluctance, force is necessary to hold back the chaos which injustice and the irrational element in man threaten to make of the world. But having said that, all is not lost and there is hope. Even in the failure of war there are springs of hope. In that great war play by Shakespeare, Henry V says: 'There is some soul of goodness in things evil, would men observingly distil it out.' People are mourning on both sides of this conflict. In our prayers we shall quite rightly remember those who are bereaved in our own country and the relations of the young Argentinian soldiers who were killed. Common sorrow could do something to reunite those who were engaged in this struggle. A shared anguish can be a bridge of reconciliation. Our neighbours are indeed like us.

I have had an avalanche of letters and advice about this service. Some correspondents have asked 'why drag God in?' as if the intention was to wheel up God to endorse some particular policy or attitude rather than another. The purpose of prayer and of services like this is very different and there is hope for the world in the difference. In our prayers we come into the presence of the living God. We come with our very human emotions, pride in achievement and courage, grief at loss and waste. We come as we are and not just mouthing opinions and thanksgiving which the fashion of the moment judges acceptable. As we pour into our prayer our mourning, our pride, our shame and our convictions, which will inevitably differ from person to person, if we are really present and really reaching out to God and not just demanding his endorsement, then God is able to work upon us. He is able to deepen and enlarge our compassion and to purify our thanksgiving. The parent who comes mourning the loss of a son may find here consolation, but also a spirit which enlarges our compassion to include all those Argentinian parents who have lost sons.

Man without God finds it difficult to achieve this revolution inside himself. But talk of peace and reconciliation is just fanciful and theoretical unless we are prepared to undergo such a revolution. Many of the reports I have heard about the troops engaged in this war refer to moments when soldiers have been brought face to face with what is fundamental in life and have found new sources of strength and compassion even in the midst of conflict. Ironically, it has sometimes been those spectators who remained at home, whether supporters or opponents of the conflict, who continue to be most violent in their attitudes and untouched in their deepest selves.

Man without God is less than man. In meeting God, a man is shown his failures and his lack of integrity, but he is also given strength to turn more and more of his life and actions into love and compassion for other men like himself. It is necessary to the continuance of life on this planet that more and more people make this discovery. We have been given the choice. Man possesses the power to obliterate himself, sacrificing the whole race on the altar of some God-substitute. Or he can choose life in partnership with God the Father of all. I believe that there is evidence that more and more people are waking up to the realization that this crucial decision peers us in the face here and now.

Cathedrals and churches are always places into which we bring human experiences – birth, marriage, death, our flickering communion with God, our fragile relationships with each other, so that they may be deepened and directed by the spirit of Christ. Today we bring our mixture of thanksgiving, sorrows and aspirations for a better ordering of this world. Pray God that he may purify, enlarge and redirect these in the ways of his kingdom of love and peace. Amen.

Just and Unjust Wars

🔲🔲🔲🔲

'WAR AS A method of settling international disputes is incompatible with the teaching and example of Our Lord.'[1] This resolution was passed in 1930, when Anglican bishops from all over the world gathered in London for the Lambeth Conference. In subsequent decades, the Lambeth bishops have reiterated that judgement and that is where I wish to begin. War is always a failure. It would be a mistake to understand my title in a complacent sense. The 'just war' tradition does not legitimize war as such. It rather seeks to prevent wars and has a built-in reluctance to resort to the use of force.

It is an essential precondition to thought about war in a Christian context to appreciate the biblical insistence that we live in a world in rebellion against its own best interests – a world which has rejected the order given to it by its creator. War is a vivid sign of this rebellion. Our world is marked by a yearning for unity and harmony but it is also disfigured by endemic conflict in which one man or group seeks to dominate others.

Christian thought has not lacked realism about the intransigence of conflict. Christians have usually argued that in what they regard as an interim world, force may be necessary to restrain the violent and protect the weak from injustice. There is in our faith a hope for the future but no naiveté about the present. Men of principle, men who have known what is best for their neighbours, have wrought havoc in our world. But the alternative of mere pragmatism is not enough. The ethics of the Kingdom are a judgement on the inescapable limitations both of ideology and pragmatism. The Pope said, 'War should belong to the tragic past, to history', but we have to deal with the fact that it is

[1] Lecture to the Royal Institute of International Affairs, Chatham House, 25 January 1983

manifestly a part of the tragic present as well. In that present of ours two symbols of hope and fear have been burned into the consciousness of our contemporaries – the planet and the cloud. By 'the planet' I mean the earth, sapphire-blue and beautiful, photographed and seen whole for the first time from the moon. By 'the cloud' I mean the mushroom-shaped cloud over Hiroshima.

The vision of the earth as a whole is a symbol of the essential unity of our planet. It has already helped to heighten our perception of a world made one by the interdependence of its economy, the new possibilities of global communication and the problems of pollution and energy which cannot be solved by individual states and which demand a common response. At no time in history has it seemed more realistic, and necessary, to regard the world as a unity. The cloud, however, is a reminder not only of the intransigence of conflict but also of the volcanic forces which threaten to tear the world apart. We now have the power to destroy civilizations which have been painfully constructed over thousands of years. This terrible power has to be managed. It cannot be disinvented.

The biblical tradition puts a heavy emphasis on the management of power. God is seen at work, bringing order to the elements of creation. 'He gave to the sea his decree that the waters should not pass his commandment . . . he appointed the foundations of the earth' (Prov. 8.29). Some Christian treatments of conflict neglect this inheritance and see power as primarily something to be renounced. This is a dangerous oversimplification, which often arises from a refusal to distinguish between the ethics appropriate to a private individual within society and those applying to competent authorities – in our case, mainly sovereign states. The Old Testament is insistent that we have a responsibility for seeking justice and the well-being of creatures in the world as it exists. It is in no doubt that force may be used to ensure the preservation of these ends.

While the New Testament is not primarily concerned about the right use of power, even in the Sermon on the Mount Matthew takes care to set the whole discourse in the context of the Old Testament law. He does this in words he attributes directly to Jesus: 'Think not that I am come to destroy the law . . . whosoever therefore shall break one of these least commandments and shall teach men so, he shall be called the least in the Kingdom of Heaven.' (Matt. 5.17,19). Even though he was speaking to the Jewish people before the inauguration of the Church, it is clear that Jesus accepted the law as God-given. What our Lord goes on to say cannot be taken in any way to undermine the law's concern for the responsible use of power to preserve justice and freedom.

I underline this point because some Christians would deny that there was any possibility of 'just' war and would claim that Christianity was not compatible with any support for the use of force and was essentially pacifist. Bonhoeffer, the German martyr to Hitler's tyranny who wrote a book, *The Cost of Discipleship*, advocating total renunciation of personal rights because of the Sermon on the Mount, had to struggle with this problem. Finally he came to accept that evil must be combated. One may renounce one's own rights. One cannot renounce one's responsibility for preserving the rights of others.

The Christian must respect the world of law and limit. In our contemporary world, he must be concerned with sovereign states and how they use their power, but in certain repects, as we shall see later, a Christian can never rest content with the provisional kind of peace which can be guaranteed by states. The way indicated by our Lord transcends the world of law and limit, but recognizes it as a condition of the discovery of a richer kind of God-given peace.

Order is a precondition of spiritual development. The Christian tradition, however, shares with many others the conviction that no order is stable unless it is founded in justice. Wars undertaken to defend order must be subject to the scrutiny of justice. There must be a just reason for resorting to war and the conflict must be conducted by just means. Before I look rather more closely at what those statements mean in practice, I am conscious that some who would call themselves 'realists' deny that such considerations *can* have weight or meaning in war. War, they would argue, dissolves moral meanings and it is only possible to understand what is going on if moral talk is translated into a sober analysis of conflicting interests.

When I was a lecturer with Swan's Hellenic Cruises, I several times had the privilege of standing in the ruins of the theatre of Melos and recalling the encounter between the Athenian generals and the Melian oligarchs. Thucydides puts into the mouth of the generals a speech as unvarnished as any realist could wish. 'We will make use of no fair phrases . . . what is just is arrived at in human arguments only when the necessity on both sides is equal and the powerful exact what they can while the weak yield what they must.' Despite such straight talking, the islanders refused to submit, looking for aid from their allies. Eventually, however, the Athenians, as they had predicted, were triumphant and either massacred or enslaved the populace. This success, however, was an ominous prelude to the disastrous Sicilian expedition in which the Athenians overreached themselves and were humiliated. It was the turning-point of the whole war. I do not believe that governments and human societies can survive for very long without at least appearing to themselves to respect the claims of justice.

A more recent example was the My-Lai massacre. The shock generated by this incident was a tribute to the moral sensitivity of Americans. It played a part in demoralizing both soldiers and public opinion at home. They were prepared to accept the necessary sacrifices only as long as they believed that they were fighting in a just cause and that there was justice in the conduct of a war.

Christian thinkers, notably St Augustine and St Thomas Aquinas, borrowed, largely from Stoic sources, a language with which to analyze the question of justice and war and over the past 1000 years a so-called 'just war' theory has been elaborated. There are many easily accessible accounts of this tradition, so I do not intend to do much more before this expert audience than to remind you of its chief components. For a fuller treatment, which is still pithy and lucid, I would recommend a document produced recently by the Roman Catholic bishops of the United States: *The Challenge of Peace*. This important pamphlet is the second draft of a proposed pastoral letter.

The theory falls into two parts: the *jus ad bellum* and the *jus in bello*. It has to be established that there is justice in the resort to force, sufficient to override a brutally realistic view of the moral ugliness of war. Those who go to war must also not only have a reasonable hope of success, but they should also believe that the damage to be inflicted and the cost in lives lost and wasted resources will be proportionate to the good to be gained by taking up arms. When the war actually begins, this principle of proportionality should continually be applied along with the principle of discrimination, which prohibits all actions directly aimed at killing non-combatants.

By these criteria, very few wars are 95 per cent just on one side and in the same degree unjust on the other. In my judgement, the Second World War approximates, as near as may be, to a just war. The Germans claimed that theirs was a just cause, basing their case on the injustices of the Versailles settlement. This was a pretence, however, and not supported by another principle in *jus ad bellum*: right intention. In Hitler's mouth, these claims were a cloak for war aims totally unjust and inhuman. Even so, the justice of the Allied cause contained some ambiguous elements. If the war was so right in 1939, why was it not undertaken sooner, in 1936 for example, when more resolute action might even have stopped Hitler in his tracks and avoided the pain of Czechoslovakia being sacrificed? More awkward by far, there is a question which presses upon all of us who were taught during the war and in the years after to regard Hitler's tyranny as by any standards worse than Stalin's. How has it been 'better for humanity' that Hitler's demonic regime was eliminated at the cost of reinforcing and extending Stalin's?

Nevertheless, I am convinced that the Second World War comes as close as anything to a just cause, although there were some events within it which are difficult to justify on *jus in bello* criteria. It is always important to recognize that war is inevitably a mixture of accident, personalities, moral coarseness, pure tragedy and that just war contains these elements as well. Despite these ambiguities, the categories and principles of the just war tradition do help us in the necessary business of educating the Christian conscience in making moral judgements about the right use of force.

It is too soon to extract all the lessons from the Falklands conflict, but in the light of the just war tradition I still think that it was right to send a task force after the Argentinian invasion because it was necessary that aggression should not be permitted to short-circuit the processes of negotiation. I also believe that there was justice in the conduct of the war and general respect for the principles of discrimination and minimum force. But, as I said at the time, it was, and is, important to count the cost at every stage. The principle of proportionality demands that we measure the immediate damage inflicted and the cost incurred against the good intended by taking up arms, but today we must also, in an interdependent world, reflect on the wider consequences for the international community.

Although this way of thinking may be a useful tool for helping us to form moral judgements about the so-called 'conventional' wars which continue to distract the world – wars like that between Iran and Iraq and the Soviet operations in Afghanistan as well as the revolutionary struggles in Southern Africa and Central America – I am convinced that full-scale nuclear war cannot possibly qualify as a just war. Here we come to a real difficulty of maintaining the distinction in my title in a nuclear age. There could not be any *jus in bello* in either full-scale nuclear or biological war, because it would be impossible to discriminate between combatants and noncombatants. I have children and the elderly particularly in mind. Also, the scale of the destruction inflicted on both sides would inevitably nullify any good intended by entering the war. There is no such thing as just mutual obliteration.

Human history has been full of just and unjust wars, but since 1945 we have been confronted with the possibility of a kind of warfare which is, soberly speaking, madness. What are we to do? We are faced at present with the problem of how to get from where we all know we are, in a world capable of destroying itself, to where we all want to be, in a world where conflict is channelled into creative directions and where potentially lethal power is used to improve the life of mankind.

The cloud over Hiroshima has signalled the beginning of a period dominated by the existence of a potential for a kind of war which cannot possibly be just. We ought not to be complacent about such a situation. If retention of nuclear weapons can be justified at all, then more urgency has to be shown in stabilizing the situation. We are faced with the twin dangers of vertical proliferation as the overkill capacity of the existing nuclear arsenals is developed and the horizontal proliferation represented by the increase in the number of states capable of initiating nuclear war.

One of the most horrifying aspects of the present situation is the apparent placid acceptance of the dangerous *status quo*. When disarmament initiatives are produced by whatever government, it is frightening to hear the immediate dismissive responses. It is becoming incredible to write off every Soviet suggestion as a propaganda ploy. To do so underestimates the extent to which everyone has an interest in seeing the present tensions relaxed. As the Pope has said in his message to the United Nations' Special Session on Disarmament, there must be 'an immediate and urgent struggle by governments to reduce progressively and equally their armaments'. The Pope properly includes so-called conventional armaments as well. I am particularly concerned about the effects of the international arms trade, but a first priority must be the reduction of the dependence on nuclear weapons to a minimum level compatible with national security. There must be progress to a mutual, verifiable nuclear disarmament between world powers.

I do not despair of negotiations in the present climate. Responsible public pressure is denting unpardonable complacency about this issue in the countries where public opinion is free to express itself. This is not, alas, happening to the same extent in the Soviet Union. But even there a perception of the danger from the cloud which faces us all is reinforced by the economic difficulties and the competition for limited resources.

A measure of disarmament is, however, only one side of the picture. The cloud represents the outcome of man's attempt over hundreds of years to manage and dominate his environment and to impose himself upon nature and his fellows. Ironically, the effort to achieve mastery has brought us to a point where we have unbound unmanageable forces. We do not know for certain (with only the experience of Hiroshima and Nagasaki to go by) how far-reaching the effect of a nuclear war would be on the genetic future of mankind, or how irreversible the damage to our planet. The cloud is a judgement on centuries of aggressive intention. But perhaps, if the significance of the cloud is properly understood and accepted, there is hope here as well as fear. Curiously, in the Bible the cloud is a sign of God's presence: 'He spake unto them out of the cloudy pillar' (Ps. 99.7).

This is a moment to seek not only to stabilize as far as possible the balance of terror, but to gain fresh determination to build more effective international institutions to reflect our perception of one world, as seen in the photograph of the sapphire planet. World government may not be as utopian for those born after 1945 as it seems to be for those of us who were born before, but for the moment I am not thinking so much of world government as of a new world order. I think that we should be paying more attention to the plea contained in the first report, issued in September 1982, of the new Secretary-General of the United Nations, Señor Perez de Cuellar. He described what he called 'the new international anarchy' and listed some steps which governments ought urgently to consider: greater use of the United National mediation facilities; more immediate resort to the Security Council and the building up of the United Nations' policing capability. The Secretary-General is talking about the provision of arrangements for the world which are possessed by the humblest local authority – an ambulance, a fire brigade, a police force.

There is, of course, nothing new in the concept. The United Nations has already advanced much further here than the old League. But it is strange that the subject is so neglected in comparison with disarmament. Peacekeeping operations have proliferated outside the United Nations in the last three years: in Zimbabwe, in Sinai and now in Beirut. These seem to me to be important victories for peace on the road to some kind of world order.

A new world order is not, of course, only a matter of a more efficient police force. We should not forget the contention of the Brandt Commission that the denial of justice to the hungry and poor in the world will have more and more explosive consequences from which none of us will be entirely insulated. This is another way in which we should seek to develop the capacity to feel and act as world citizens. It is not that we have to abandon a patriotic love for our own homeland, but we should try to transcend national self-interest as a determinant of policy.

There are, however, so many barriers to our sympathy and compassion; so many stereotypes of one another that make talk of brotherhood merely theoretical. The Pope's New Year message emphasized the importance of a commitment to 'dialogue' as a way of reducing the dangerous misunderstandings and tensions generated by our ignorance of, and contempt for, one another. I have had some experience of theological conversations with Russian churchmen and as a consequence I have come to glimpse the differences between our mental furniture and basic categories of thought. It seems worse than ironic that we are running down Russian studies in our schools and universities just at a time when we are increasing our defence spending.

But peace is not just something for high-powered dialogue or international commissions. We have to acknowledge that the springs of violence and war are in everybody. This is implied in the UNESCO constitution, 'since wars begin in the minds of men, it is in the minds of men that the defences of peace must be constructed'. There is a brand of easy talk about peace which promotes cynicism. The world is awash with references to 'the peace-loving peoples' which make one wonder how the relatively small numbers of people in the Pentagon and the Kremlin can actually impose their will upon the rest of us. Tolstoy was rather more realistic when he said 'the great mass of men . . . are hypnotized into war by their governments in the first instance but alas and even more remarkably, by each other'.

To do anything about the violence in each one of us is to go beyond the world of law and limits represented in the time of Christ by the government of the Roman Empire. Wars and conflicts arise in a world which yearns in its smallest particles for union and relationship, because that principle is confronted by another in which the individual parts of the world strive for mastery over one another when they should be looking for marriage. The way of renouncing power and the lust for mastery, which is the way of Jesus Christ, is one that is being followed even now by many people in the Christian world. But this way demands a profound and costly personal repentance and sometimes even peace groups can manifest the kind of unrepentant and unreflective aggression they so readily ascribe to others. Few have the wisdom of Gandhi who, when he was discussing with the British government in India the use of violence by the government against the Indians, stressed that the violence in the heart of the Indian people and of himself contributed to the overall violence of the conflict. But the way of renouncing power and subjecting self-interest to the interest of others must be pursued if the peace intended by God is to be established. This path, however, can only be trodden in the context of and perhaps partly in reaction to a world which has first been restrained and ordered by law and limits.

I believe myself to be a preacher of the Kingdom of God to which our Lord pointed supremely when he said, 'My Kingdom is not of this world', and also I pray those mysterious words, 'Thy Kingdom come, on Earth as it is in Heaven'. The road to the realization of this Kingdom is heavily mined and we have to tread carefully, defusing the mines one by one.

The Third World: A Christian Concern

🔲🔲🔲🔲

I HOPE THAT what I have to say to you today[1] will reach you not because it is being said by an archbishop but because it is true and because it demands a response.

I should like to start with a brief word for those who say that churchmen should keep out of the political arena by pointing out what Christians have achieved by getting involved. For example, in 1941, my predecessor as Archbishop of Canterbury, William Temple, convened the Malvern Conference. The purpose of that meeting was described as 'to consider what are the fundamental facts which are directly relevant to the new society that is emerging and how Christian thought can be shaped to play a leading part in reconstruction following the war' – an ambitious agenda – the sort of thing which might be dubbed in the clichés of our own day, 'trendy rhetoric'.

After the conference, Temple gathered around him at Lambeth a number of leading economists, and the book *Christianity and Social Order* was published. In that work, now of course somewhat dated, but very influential at the time, Temple pointed out that religion must be concerned with the total life of society, including economics and politics. To those who accused him of stepping into highly technical matters, he replied that as a Christian he had an obligation to support the cause of the underprivileged and if they were to be supported, then this meant working for economic reform.

That is an example from this country and from the past: but today we are hearing its echoes in relation to our understanding of the world as a whole. Over the last few years, and particularly since the publication of the Brandt

[1] Speech at a seminar on Our Response to the Poorest of the Third World, arranged by the Commission for International Justice and Peace, Archbishop's House, Westminster, 23 November 1982

Report, the Churches and the development lobbies have gained a maturity and a professionalism which have been lacking in the past. Those of us in positions of influence must cultivate this deepening awareness of the need for hard work as well as heart-stretching rhetoric.

Why should this assertion of Christian principle be applied to the world stage, urgently at this time?

I think the answer to this lies in the concept of brotherhood, which I would argue is central to the Christian faith. In the battle against the slave trade, the eighteenth-century principle of individual human rights and the utilitarians' doctrine of the greatest good for the greatest number played their parts, but in this country a major imperative came from evangelicals like Wilberforce and their poster of a black man with the caption, 'I am a Man and a Brother'. If you view the world from the understanding that all men and women are brothers and sisters, you find that the religious vision is now being substantiated by the way our world is developing. I can pick up my telephone in Lambeth Palace and talk to the Archbishop of Nigeria – or Japan, or Australia, or the Solomon Islands.

No great religion, least of all Christianity, has ever suggested that moral obligations begin and end with the citizens of one particular state at one particular time: and I find it heartening that there is, and especially among young people, a great and growing consciousness that the gross disparities between our own affluent, developed nations and those of the struggling southern hemisphere are not just a threat to our own still comparatively cosy economic order. Our rising generation is the first to have grown up with a view of planet earth from the outside: the photographs of our beautiful planet, taken from outer space, are not, as perhaps they are to older generations, just symbols of technological advance. They show the world from beyond the artificial barriers which man in his ignorance and greed has created. They have lived with this vision of the world in its entirety and they have seen no reason why it should not be beautiful for all who dwell upon it.

Forty years later, the essential principle that Temple stood for has not changed. Those who would follow Christ are obliged to support the weak, the poor and the deprived:

in the words of Cardinal Hume, speaking in Cologne three weeks ago, 'We need to see the unbreakable connection between love of God and love of our neighbour'. The establishment of this connection must lead to the conclusion that parallel to the pursuit of brotherhood is the pursuit of justice for *all* those embraced by the fatherhood of God and this brotherhood of man. This is a principle which is, in the words of our time, non-negotiable.

Have all those who call themselves Christian lived up to this ideal? The answer, of course, is No; but many *have* sacrificed their lives to the service of the less fortunate, and it is they who have done so in the past, and who are doing so today, who give me the moral authority to be here today and to tell you, in their name, what we, as people of influence in our various fields, must do if we are to call ourselves Christians. We may not be called to follow particular examples of service in the field; but from wherever they are – from the islands of Indonesia to the mountains of Nepal, from the plains of Uganda to the forests of Brazil – they look to us to support their work, and they look for many kinds of support because there are many ways of demonstrating a Christian concern.

For many people, this may mean raising money through a church jumble sale. For others, it will mean running classes and discussion groups to arouse greater public awareness of the work which needs to be done. For others still, support will be mainly vocal. The mass lobby of Parliament on 5 May 1981 which ensured that the subject of world development reached the political agenda and could no longer be ignored by any serious politician, was due almost entirely to efforts by the Churches, and 80 per cent of the people who supported that lobby were active Christians.

These activities at home, and the truly remarkable achievements of Christians working all over the world – often working, I might add, in the most distressing and dangerous conditions – give us the right to be heard on these issues. I am here today not as a vague voice delivering a pocketful of rhetoric from some ecclesiastical ivory tower, but as the proud representative of many thousands who work to fulfil their obligations as Christians not just in organizations which carry Christian labels – such as Christian Aid – but in more neutral agencies also: the Save the Children Fund is an obvious example.

Part of the obligation of being a Christian is that of saying aloud what you believe to be right, and I make no apologies for it. The admission of Christian concern must lead to a proper study of the issues to which that concern is applied: Christians must not allow themselves to be fobbed off by those who claim a monopoly of technical knowledge, nor by those who simply refuse to listen.

If we want people to take us seriously, we must ensure that we are properly prepared. I think I am right in saying that the Zulu chieftains had a favourite order of battle, known as the horns of the buffalo because it involved launching a two-pronged attack on an enemy, to take him on both flanks at once. The horns of the Christian buffalo are those of sound knowledge and clear moral authority.

I would like now to look at the implications of Christian concern for official policy towards the developing nations.

We are all aware of the problems of our own western economies, and that the resolution of our economies will do much to assist those of developing countries. I am glad that in a very difficult economic situation the Government has not resorted to the kind of siege mentality, restrictions on overseas investment and import quotas which would further damage the international economy.

Resisting demands for protectionism is extremely important to Third World countries; and for the wealthier of the developing countries in particular, private finance and investment has a vital role to play. By 1980 private flows from Britain to developing countries totalled £4800 million. Combined official and private flows for that year were about £5.5 billion or about 2.5 per cent of our Gross National Product. This is well above the United Nations target figure of 1 per cent. This is pleasing and it is to be regretted that we cannot meet the other main target, that of 0.7 per cent of Gross National Product, for official development assistance. There are, I am assured, good *technical* reasons for the fall in Britain's official aid performance; from 0.52 per cent of Gross National Product in 1979 to 0.34 per cent in 1980. We should also be doing ourselves an injustice if we were to ignore our trade flows, which are some twenty times larger than official aid flows. I apologize for throwing these figures at you. I am fearful of joining what the Minister for Overseas Development has called the 'pocket-calculator brigade'. I am sure you will already be familiar with them; but they form an important background to the increasing concern which many in this work here voiced to me about present attitudes to development issues, and the whole way in which the matter of official aid is being approached.

One of the present Government's much quoted intentions in the development field is 'to give greater weight in the allocation of aid to political, industrial and commercial considerations alongside basic development objectives'. There is much debate about how effective government to government aid can be under certain circumstances, and I admit that I have seen some of the dangers at first hand in Africa and Asia, but aid tied to commercial or political considerations will inevitably be constrained by exactly those considerations. It is obviously vital that British firms win foreign orders and contracts, and sometimes they may need government assistance in order to do so. But in my view it would be absolutely wrong were that assistance in any form whatsoever to be taken out of the aid budget. Doubtless the country so assisted benefits, but where assistance is given partly in order to preserve jobs here at home – effectively a form of government subsidy – then the funds should come from the Department of Industry, not from the Overseas Development Administration. We must insist that funds earmarked for genuine development purposes are not swallowed up in disguised subsidies. Trade and aid, even when they serve the same ultimate purpose, are two different matters and they must not be confused.

Of course trade is vital and of course constructive trade assists development, but perhaps we have become over-obsessed with development at the expense of basic humanitarian aid. This possibility was brought home to me by one aid worker who is concerned particularly with government funding of health and welfare projects. He said: 'The idea of welfare for its own sake has gone out of the window. It's development or nowt.'

I sense a real crisis of confidence among those who work in the development field. Not only do they feel hamstrung by the lack of resources, but they feel that they must battle constantly against official lack of support. The Government will protest that this is not the case, and that it is genuinely and wholeheartedly committed to world development. The point I must make to you is that the standard bearers in the aid agencies *do feel* deserted, that their support has dwindled to nothing and even gone into reverse. The government figures may counter this view, but moral support is always as vital as material support: and you can cut off that moral support either directly, by restraining your commitment to aid; or indirectly, by, for instance, phasing out all government funding for development education. The withdrawal of funds from the Centre for World Development Education, from 1984, is a particularly sad case: yet another example of a small organization which, if it does not just close down, will have to expend valuable time and energy on fund-raising. If a government makes these kinds of cuts, it takes more than rhetoric to restore lost time, lost programmes, lost effort and lost confidence.

The Churches' involvement in development education is very considerable, so I can speak about it with the confidence which comes from belonging to an institution with a relatively clear conscience.

There are a number of steps which might rectify these growing suspicions of official indifference. There is an overall need for the Government to express its commitment to the poorer nations without throwing up at the same time a smoke-screen of caveats and qualifications. That commitment might well be clearer, for example, if the Minister for Overseas Development was in the Cabinet – not a purely cosmetic change, but so that he may defend and support the aid vote in times of financial stringency. I have already mentioned the need to support development education in order to achieve greater public acceptance for overseas aid. I would also expect the present Government, with its commitment to and emphasis upon private initiative, to increase substantially its support for non-governmental aid agencies. I would also like to commend private ventures such as the International Broadcasting

Trust, which, over the coming year, will do more for development education among ordinary people than any other single effort. I look forward to the day when, through the efforts of those who seek to arouse the public conscience, overseas aid becomes an election issue. It is already the case in the Netherlands and perhaps other places in Western Europe. I feel that day may be nearer than some politicians seem to realize, and the Government would do well to look again at the conclusions of the Report of the all-party Foreign Affairs Committee which was published in July 1982, and to rethink the response to them, especially where they relate to development education.

But I have a still more fundamental concern yet, and this is that we, as a society, represented by our Government, have yet to take on board the enormity of the developing world's problems. There are some figures which are simply too large to be entered on the screen of the average pocket calculator: the 800-odd million people, for example, who, in the words of Robert MacNamara, are living 'in situations so deprived as to be below any rational definition of human decency'; or the 17 million children who die each year – many of whom could be saved by the expedition of relatively small sums on basic health care.

The simple fact is that we are in danger of becoming moral abstainers. Of course Britain's aid flows, public and private, are not inconsiderable; of course they compare rather well even with those of much richer countries and are positively generous compared with the efforts of some countries. But this is to miss the point. The fact is that we simply do not give enough, in absolute or relative terms, to those who need our help. Many noble noises are made, but when the organ stops the collection plate remains rather bare.

This is a bleak note on which to end, but I cannot in all honesty do otherwise: for at least half the population of the planet, the world is a very bleak place. By ignoring the moral dimensions of the problems we risk making it bleaker still, and for ourselves also.

Homosexuality

🔲🔲🔲🔲

THE GLOUCESTER REPORT[1] has not received a very warm welcome from those who would like the Church to sound a clear blast on the trumpet on either side of this argument. But at the very least I believe that the authors of the Report deserve congratulations for the way in which they have skilfully marshalled medical and social data to explode prejudices still commonly maintained. I hope the Report will be used to promote the kind of informed discussion which will combat the silly insinuations and innuendoes, the casual contempt for and unthinking mockery of homosexuality which so often pass for discussion of the subject even, alas, in church circles. Often in, for example, the field of race relations or care of the handicapped, we are able to point to an evolution in public attitudes and understanding. I am not sure that this is so in the public discussion of homosexuality. I think the situation may even have deteriorated since the nineteenth century.

It was about 1897 when the word homosexual was first used as a noun by the psychiatrist Havelock Ellis and he apologized for such bad usage. Until then people spoke of homosexual acts and not homosexual persons, and this was one of the reasons why students and others in the nineteenth century could write letters to one another with expressions of affection few would dare to use today.

Once we were encouraged by Freud to define people in terms of their sexual feelings, the danger was there of tyrannically imposing the categories *heterosexual* and *homosexual* on a range of relationships and feelings which cannot be categorized in such a banal and crude way. One of the results has been the eclipse of friendship as a profound spiritual relationship which inspired some of the greatest

[1] Statement in the debate on Homosexual Relationships, General Synod, 27 February 1981

art and writing in the ancient world. I detect much ungenerous suspicion surrounding friendship in our own day and I am reminded of that passage in C. S. Lewis in which he pleads with us not to judge close relations between persons of the same sex by any crude *a priori* theory:

> Kisses, tears and embraces are not in themselves evidence of homosexuality. Hrothgar embracing Beowulf, Johnson embracing Boswell (a pretty flagrantly heterosexual couple) and all those hairy old toughs of centurions in Tacitus, clinging to one another and begging for last kisses when the legion was broken up . . . all pansies? If you can believe that you can believe anything . . . It is, of course, not the demonstrative gestures of friendship among our ancestors but the absence of such gestures in our own society that calls for some special explanation.

Just as I would deprecate automatic suspicion attaching to friendship, so on the other side I cannot but believe that those who are obsessive about so-called gay rights contribute to this unhealthy atmosphere.

I have no doubt that people will refer to the matter of clergy discipline. One of my rule-of-thumb tests for ordination would be that if a man was so obsessive a campaigner on this subject that it made his ministry unavailable to the majority of church people, then I would see no justification in ordaining him.

To deprecate the casual and unthinking talk about homosexuality does not mean that we should abandon any moral judgement on the subject altogether or accommodate ourselves to echo contemporary judgement. Our contemporaries are divided on this subject and if we have anything to offer to the debate we must start from the Church's Scriptures, its title deeds and its traditional teaching. The Report, however, does very clearly illustrate the new climate in which we must seek to interpret our tradition.

The Church itself is not united on this subject and I should like briefly to sketch, as I see it, the four main points of view, indicating my own preference.

First, some people see homosexuality simply as a sin and make much of the Sodom story. Even those, however, who still think in this way have to learn not to judge other people's temptations. Second, some see homosexuality as sickness and feel it may be catching. Those who still think in this way must have the obligation of exercising compassion.

And then, third, it is possible to see homosexuality neither as sin nor sickness but as handicap, a state with which people have to cope, with limitations and hardships in which the fulfilment of heterosexual love and marriage are denied. If you take this view, to which I myself incline, it has a very important consequence for your attitude. We are learning to treat the handicapped not with pity, but with deep respect and an awareness that often through their handicap they can obtain a degree of self-giving and compassion which is denied to those not similarly afflicted.

The last point of view, which is widespread, is the one that sees homosexuality as a minority but valid alternative to the heterosexual way followed by the majority. With the authors of the Gloucester Report, I do not believe that it is possible for anyone to be loyal to the Christian tradition and to see homosexual and heterosexual relations as having equal validity.

The Report has been derided for not being definite enough. The caution shown by the authors seems to me to be courageous and responsible in view of new evidence, both medical and social, and new ways of evaluating the evidence.

The best way forward now, I would suggest, is for the Church to combat with vigour the hatred and denigration of homosexuals which is widespread in our society and to try to come to a balanced understanding of their difficulties and their potential by seeing it not as a sin or as a sickness, but more as a handicap, always bearing in mind the new ways in which we have come to view those who are handicapped, and to learn from them.

The Pursuit of Justice

🔲🔲🔲🔲

'THE PURSUIT OF Justice'[1] conjures up images of a quest or some perilous hunt: not of a small animal like a fox but of something unpredictable that might turn and rend you. One is reminded of Macaulay:

> All shrank like boys who unaware
> Ranging the woods to start a hare
> Came to the mouth of the dark lair
> Where growling low, a fierce old bear
> Lay amidst bones and blood.

Human Rights and Justice: Origins

The suggestion that justice is always beyond us, waiting to be more fully disclosed as we pursue it, is true to history. Our vision of what constitutes justice has changed throughout history and never has the transformation been greater than over the past four centuries. The seventeenth-century merchant saw little injustice in the slave trade which by the nineteenth century was abhorrent. The pursuit and exploration of justice in the seventeenth, eighteen and early nineteenth centuries was preoccupied with individual political rights and liberties – freedom for the individual from the oppression of governments. In the nineteenth century, however, and even more in the earlier part of our own century, the concept of justice has been expanded to embrace the questions of social disadvantage and economic deprivation.

In considering therefore the dynamic enterprise which is the pursuit of justice we are looking for a vocabulary, a grammar, a structure of concepts which will assist us in our quest and which will reveal a more and more generous vision of justice. This vision should extend to and help us to

[1] Lecture at St George's House, Windsor Castle, 10 April 1981

realize our obligations to those who suffer poverty and hunger throughout the Third World, those who are denied freedom of speech in repressive regimes and those who are still unborn. We are also looking for a vocabulary of justice which will command assent globally and which will be capable of providing a framework within which nations of very different cultures may compose their differences without resort to war. In a dangerous world where wars can be waged with unprecedented destructiveness our search for the justice which brings peace ought to be urgent and strenuous.

One of the most frequently evoked vocabularies and conceptual schemes devised to put flesh on justice is assembled around the term 'human rights'. Those who promote human rights talk argue that it provides the most hopeful and persuasive contemporary way of pursuing justice. It is the fashionable phrase nowadays in any consideration of justice. When I was Bishop of St Albans I used to be fascinated by the story of the first British martyr and tried to pass on my fascination to others. He was someone, you remember, who protected a hunted Christian priest, donned his clothes and enabled the priest to escape. Yet to the average visitor and tourist he seems a distant and shadowy figure. In recent years, with pardonable exaggeration, I used to describe him as the first who made a stand for human rights – he protected someone who was being bullied by officialdom. The allusion turned Alban into a contemporary and someone worth hearing about. I want to examine this claim for him through my lecture and to organize my exploration of the widening horizon of justice by reference to the origins, the achievements and the deficiencies of human rights talk.

The tradition of articulating justice in terms of individual rights, not just by reference to what is right, is a venerable one with its roots in medieval scholasticism. It was in the seventeenth century, however, in the work of men like Grotius at the beginning of the century and Locke at its close, that a systematic notion of justice was evolved with the modern idea of individual rights at its centre. To put his case with outrageous simplicity, Locke asserted that injustice may be defined in terms of the denial of rights, while justice requires that certain natural rights which belong to individuals should be respected at all costs.

Human Rights and Justice: Achievements

The achievements of this way of understanding justice over the two centuries following Locke are obvious. These achievements amount to a vivid illustration of the power contained in new ways of talking about a subject like justice which has been so thoroughly discussed from Plato to the present day. Locke elaborated a way of talking about justice which revealed new facets of what was just or unjust and harnessed a new passion and certainty to the pursuit of these new horizons.

Locke, in his essay on toleration, used his analysis of justice, in terms of inalienable natural rights, to provide a theoretical basis for the liberty of the individual conscience to dissent from the religious establishment, which became one of the most cherished rights of the Englishman. Barely 150 years before the time of Locke it was almost inconceivable that anyone could have the right to dissent in religious matters. It was believed that to admit such a right would be to sign the death warrant of the kingdom, since a house divided against itself cannot stand. This proved not to be the case and the consolidation of a right to religious dissent has enriched the life of this country and even brought a religious vitality and energy to the established Church itself.

The Elizabethan Settlement in the sixteenth century identified citizen and churchman. With the royal supremacy went conformity in religion. It was the peculiarly English solution to the religious wars which rent sixteenth-century Europe. The dissenting tradition has been a kind of loyal opposition within the religious life of this country, and we owe to its existence our freedom from the anti-Christian character of radical movements that has marked the history of our European neighbours.

Seeing justice in the terms of the rights of individuals also brought this concept to the centre of political theory which, in Locke's writings, became concerned with the rights of individuals against tyrannical governments. This important notion passes by way of the American Declaration of Independence to be expressed by President Carter in his attempts to claim for this tradition a global validity.

The creativity of this way of thinking about justice can be demonstrated in other ways. Since 'rights' are intrinsic to persons as persons and justice is overturned when they are ignored, we arrive at the idea that these rights and their enjoyment are a part of our nature, and that they are indeed human or natural rights, rights which we ought to enjoy if justice is to be upheld simply in virtue of our being human. There is clearly no room in this account of justice for treating human beings as anything but equal before the law. The logic of this concept of human rights contributed to the alteration of public sentiment about slavery. By the early nineteenth century in England the institution of slavery had come to appear barbarous and even inconceivable where, of course, previously even St Paul had accepted it without protest as part of the natural order of society.

This way of talking about justice has so coloured our conceptions that it would be easy to underestimate its creativity and the radical character of the changes which followed upon its adoption.

Another example of an area where the creativity of this tradition is still not exhausted is to be found in the extension to women in the nineteenth and twentieth centuries of some of the rights which belong to us all under Locke's theory, simply in virtue of our being human. Women in the years between 1850 and 1950 have come of age in the sight of the law; they have been deemed to have wits as well as wombs and an overwhelming number of jobs and professions are now open to them. For the first time in our history a woman can be torn between her desire to be a mother, a partner to her husband, tinker, tailor, soldier, sailor, doctor, dustman, thief, policeman. I know of this because I am married to someone who survives what the corsetry manufacturers call 'the three-way stretch' – supporting your husband, caring for the family household, and fully pursuing your own career. The story of women's rights is one on its own. It is still not over and shows that the volcanic power of this way of thinking about justice is far from spent.

Human Rights and Justice: Deficiencies

This tradition of defining justice by reference to the inalienable rights of individuals, rights which belong to them simply by virtue of being born of human parents, has, however, been challenged over the last two centuries.

In this country Hume and Bentham reacted sharply against the vocabulary of rights. They were anxious that the questions of general welfare (the greatest happiness of the greatest number) should take precedence in social legislation over the protection of individual rights. Bentham's disciple, J. S. Mill, while not abandoning a conviction about the significance of individual rights, also perceived that it might be right in the name of increasing individual liberty to restrict the liberties of some privileged members of society. It might be possible, for example, to extend the liberties of the mass of the population by applying some of the wealth of the rich to improve the social conditions, the poor housing and lack of education which prevented so many people from enjoying the full liberties which naturally belonged to them.

This accent on the importance of providing equal opportunites balanced the earlier preoccupation with individual liberties, but there were also those in the nineteenth century who sought to pursue social justice by emphasizing fraternity. Of the trinity of concepts which presided over the French Revolution, liberty, equality and fraternity, fraternity has been the concept most frequently neglected. The inspiration of the work of Lord Shaftesbury, however, sprang from a lively sense of Christian brotherhood and the sense of responsibility for one another that comes when we take seriously the truth that we are all children of the same heavenly Father. His work owed little to the tradition of individual rights and much of the work of social justice in the nineteenth century has this typically Christian inspiration although, since it was largely undertaken at a parish level and was obscured by a hail of propaganda from those hostile to the established Church, it was work that has not received recognition proportionate to its extent or importance. I shall return to the theme of fraternity later in this lecture.

The welfare work and legislation conducive to greater social and economic justice were founded on either a modification of the traditional theory of individual rights or on the surviving influence of a religious tradition of fraternity, which was much older than the talk about individual liberties.

In very recent times, however, there has been an attack on utilitarianism, with its emphasis on general welfare, and a return to a theory of individual rights in a less diluted form as the only proper basis for a society which is truly concerned with justice.

The Work of Rawls and Nozick

This new movement is associated with the names of John Rawls and Robert Nozick. The case against utilitarianism is set out with clarity and distinction in John Rawls's book *The Theory of Justice*. This book argues that theories which stress general welfare court a danger. They obscure the earlier tradition of human rights, and particularly that character-istic and valuable insight associated with the name of Immanuel Kant – that each one of us is a separate person and not just a means to the end of some other persons or person. This separateness of persons makes them inviolable, and this truth ought to be assigned an absolute centrality in our social theory. Unless this inviolability of each one of us is guaranteed in society, so the argument runs, justice will never be secured. So justice comes once again, as in the natural rights tradition, to be defined in terms of the maximizing of individual rights, which are in turn seen as liberties to act in a fashion which it would be contrary to justice to constrain. This is, I think, the essence of Rawls's account of justice, that it is a matter of assuring to each individual his or her rights, compatible with the good order of society, and leaving each person free so far as possible to pursue their own projects. 'Every person', Rawls writes, 'possesses an inviolability founded on justice that even the welfare society as a whole cannot override.' Justice, in short, is a matter of securing the right to this inviolability and enshrining it in the institutions of social life in so far as it is compatible with good order.

I believe that there are serious problems in this newly fashionable way of thinking about the relations between rights and justice. These problems illuminate the general deficiencies of the tradition of talk about rights as a way to pursue justice and to forward the creation of a truly compassionate society.

If we accept Rawls's endorsement of Kant's insight, about the inviolability of the individual person as the true centre of any talk about justice in society, then it becomes difficult to use the term human rights in anything but a very restricted sense. If it is essential to justice that the inviolability of individuals and their liberties are respected as the absolute basis of society, then it is possible, or even perhaps our duty, to insist that it must be contrary to justice to force individuals to help each other – for example, by taxing the rich to alleviate poverty among other citizens.

According to another influential contemporary theorist, Professor Robert Nozick, such a policy is indeed unjust since it uses one person as a means to another's end. Nozick's theory of the connection between rights and justice leads him to characterize all taxation as equivalent to forced labour, to making me do something for someone else that I have no duty to do, since I have the right as an inviolable individual person, separate from other persons, to insist on being left alone, and indeed this is the essence of what it means for me to be justly treated.

I am sure that most of those who invoke human rights language would want it to work for societies in which justice implied a greater sense of mutual responsibility and compassion than some current social philosophy would seem to allow. The way in which the idea of individual inviolability has become central to the discussion of the relations between rights and justice seems to empty human rights talk of much of its content.

So there has been an attempt to use the human rights vocabulary to cover the right to work, to be fed, to have security in old age; but it is in fact impossible in logic to derive something like the right to work from a doctrine of human rights. If you force someone to employ somebody else it is in fact an infringement of human rights, if human rights are derived from the paramount right of an individual to inviolability. This theory makes it possible to deny that I have the duty to aid the man fallen among thieves, since to demand this of me is to demand that I act to help others in certain ways which I may resent and find damaging to my own interest. Rescuing the victims of wayside assault takes time, money and possibly exposes me to danger. To force me to act in this way is to force me to act socially against my individual will and this is the definition of injustice. Professor Rawls and Professor Nozick underwrite the Levite's highway code!

I hope that I have sufficiently emphasized the achievements of the 'rights' philosophy of justice, but it is also vital to grasp that the greater compassion of our society towards those who need help has derived from theories explicitly opposed to the attempt to make individual rights central to social philosophy. The welfare state, for example, is founded on ideals of social justice promoted both by the utilitarian insistence on the general welfare of society and by the Christian passionate insistence on brotherhood. Even the abolition of the slave trade and slavery itself, often seen as an outstanding achievement for the Rights of Man philosophy, owed at least as much to a Christian campaign that recognized the slave as a brother. You will remember the slogan of the anti-slavery lobby which represented the black slave saying 'I am a man *and* a brother'. The Rights of Man philosophy, enshrined in the American Declaration of Independence, did not prevent the United States remaining a slave-owning society for close on a century after the revolutionary war.

You may have been expecting from me something more swashbuckling and colourful, an appeal to seek justice and ensue it, not this kind of examination of the language in which we are wont to discuss the topic. I make no apologies for the approach. The hard-headed men of affairs who dismiss theoretical or philosophical talk about such subjects as justice are usually prisoners of yesterday's philosophies and theories without knowing it.

Isaiah Berlin used to say that the object of philosophy was to waken us from lying on a bed of unexamined assumptions. Now we have a situation in which there is a contention for the heart of the great concept of justice. An old, and I believe deficient, orthodoxy has been brought up to date and could provide the basis for thought and action about social justice easily assimilable to a hard-hearted philosophy of individualism.

We are considering basic assumptions – often unexamined. I do not believe that members of governments or an establishment go on for very long without mental breakdowns, either individually or collectively, unless they have a very strong sense that they are doing justice. I am questioning the philosophical background which might give some people a sense of security in a definition of justice which is so limited that it can easily serve the selfish or the hard-hearted in their social relations both at home and abroad.

I am concerned, however, not only with the effects of this new orthodoxy on the attempt to built a compassionate society, but also with its effect upon the very coherence of society. The individualistic theory of human rights is too easily appropriated by individuals and used about their own affairs to fuel grievances and indignation. In the end this raises the problem of social cohesion and good order. We are beginning to see again in England that these things are not to be taken for granted and that the attainment of social cohesion and good order is a rare achievement in the history of the world. The current orthodoxy which puts individual rights at the centre of the pursuit of justice could hasten the disintegration which is evident in England where every day the folk becomes more like a mere aggregation of groups and individuals with conflicting claims.

I am much concerned, for the reasons which I have already stated, about the prospect for the human rights way of pursuing justice. To revert to the man fallen among thieves, it may be a mistake for us to use the vocabulary of human rights at all when considering his case. The question of whether or not the man had a right to be saved is in our society, with its characteristic presuppositions about justice, too easily answered in the negative. To demand that the priest and the Levite restrict their liberty to pass by is to show a willingness to act unjustly towards them, forgetting their inviolability as persons with liberties. They may choose to help the man, rather than leave him in the ditch, but this is not because he has any human rights that they should do this.

Reduced to these simple terms, we may all find the theory unsatisfactory and we all accept a duty to help the unfortunate man. But, when transferred to another scale, to the discussions about the millions who are close to starvation, or who are the victims of war, such theories have, I believe, hardened hearts. I rather fear that recent debates about overseas aid show that the individualist theory of justice has already brought too much comfort to the popular inclination to do little for our neighbours and brothers in other parts of the world.

Even if the man in the parable had no right to be saved, even if it could be shown that it was not contrary to justice to refrain from saving him, all that this demonstrates is that justice is not everything. We have fallen into the habit of discussing rights and justice autonomously. I believe that it is very dangerous to separate justice from its proper context. Justice is in the Christian tradition a means of expressing, in particular specific ways, the consequences of God's love for us all, the love which gives us value, and of translating the insight that we are all brothers, children of the same heavenly Father, into the terms of institutions and organizations. Reinhold Niebuhr used to say, 'Justice is the currency in which love is paid out in the world of systems and associations.'

Apart from this context and not subordinated to the great principle of love, justice can become the vehicle for demonic self-assertion which wars against community and is fed by illusions. There are no such *things* as rights in nature and to use language which teaches us to regard ourselves as possessors of natural rights rather than as the recipients of a love which gives us value, fosters destructively self-centred attitudes towards God and our fellow men. Justice must be in the service of love and this Christian conviction is, I think, largely missing from, and vital to, our contemporary social philosophies.

Much of the current talk about justice has a chilling, sometimes even a deadly, air about it. Justice is obviously central to society, but we would be right to be dismayed if our friends were just rather than kind, or our parents more just than loving. It is only an impoverished notion of justice which can survive outside the context of love.

These sentiments are, of course, difficult to combine with current talk about individuals and their rights, which can be heard as much in a professor's seminar as in the lounge bar of the Rose and Crown. But I dare to assert that it is contemporary talk about justice which is inadequate and even dangerous, not the Christian tradition or even that secular tradition which, while doubtful about its source, acknowledges the gift and the claims of love. To agree, as so many do now, that all attempts to make me help others are equally violations of my rights, is to miss the vital point that my own character has become terribly distorted if I really insist that all these rights are on a par, and thus that it is just as bad for me to be forced to give up some of my wealth for the hungry as it would be to make me undertake forced labour. Nozick, however, literally equates the two.

There has been a failure here to balance the insight that all of us ought to be recognized as separate and as having our own projects, with the truth that no man is an island entire of himself. We need to marry these truths, and I doubt whether the vocabulary of human rights is competent to perform this marriage. The chilly language of rights and justice needs to be set in the context of fraternity and a sense of the brotherhood of man. Justice needs to serve and respond to the vision of the other man that we receive when we begin to treat him as a brother.

This is no academic quibble. I believe that our present approach to justic obscures what is due from us to the national community and the world community. The very language we use, the instrument of our perceptions, distorts the picture and colludes with our selfishness to deny the obligation to help the man fallen by the wayside and the millions who are hungry. I shall be told, no doubt, that I am preferring a woolly and even sentimental account of justice to one that may be limited but is at least clear and can be turned into legislation. I resent the attempt, however, to capture the concept of justice and to confine it to a system and a language which defines injustice and wrongdoing merely as a violation of rights. What becomes of the commandment that we are to love our neighbour as ourself if we insist simply on a vocabulary of justice as conceived in terms of the protection of individual or human rights? What has been omitted is love, brotherhood, fraternity, the context and the source without which justice can come to serve demonic ends. The traditional figure of Justice, a blindfold woman wielding a sword, is meant to inspire confidence. Divorced from love, however, it can become simply terrifying.

You may feel that this attempt to bore holes in the widespread contemporary tendency to base justice simply on human rights has a thoroughly negative ring about it. I would therefore like to end by sketching briefly some of the principles on which I believe that a Christian society should be based.

A Vision of the Just Community

In Plato's *Republic*, when Socrates was asked to define justice, he replied by describing at length the sort of society in which each part would work for the good of the whole. For Plato the investigation of justice leads to an examination of the foundations of morality.

I wish to suggest that in the Christian tradition – you can find all the texts you need in the Epistle to the Romans, chapter 12 – there are four ingredients which are essential for community life. But before you judge me, wait until the end. They are all important and the beauty, as they say in the tea advertisement, is in the blend . . . as indeed it was for Plato.

First, any community worthy of the name needs what I call the family virtues – acceptance, tolerance, compassion, forgiveness. These are the qualities which provide anchorage, acceptance, companionship in a family. They enable people to grow, and without them no community will ever thrive. Care for the tender, the handicapped, the inarticulate, the child, the old, the stranger in our midst, this is basic Christianity. St Paul says: 'Weep with those who weep; rejoice with those who rejoice.'

The second ingredient is a kind of discipline of mind and spirit – the proper use of talents. The family virtues on their own can be flabby and soft, keeping people in immaturity and dependence. The welfare state becomes a nanny state. A community needs the backbone which comes from a readiness to develop our skills, set some standards, to engage in sheer hard work, undertake and stick at tiresome duties, above all to establish some principles and hold to them. St Paul again: 'There are varieties of gifts but the same Spirit.' 'Having gifts according to the measure that God has given you, you are to use them and develop them.'

The third ingredient is loyalty. Loyalty springs from pride in the community of which one is a member. It has recently had a bad name because it can be used to manipulate. It can be narrow or complacent. If so, it should be mocked; but at its best loyalty provides a nursery for our affections which need to be deepened before they can expand in scope. The noise of 60,000 Welshmen singing 'Land of my Fathers' on a Cardiff rugby ground may make the sophisticated smile, but I do not think it is displeasing to God. Communities and places, like individuals, only thrive if they are loved. That's true of a country or a company. St Paul again has it: 'We are members one of another.'

The last ingredient is again an obvious correction of the previous one. I fumble for a word, but cannot do better than 'vision', the need to look beyond the present, beyond your local loyalties to a wider world and a different future. As the Christian message has it in St Paul: 'Be not conformed to present pattern but be transformed by the renewing of your mind.' There is a need for people to know where they are going, commit themselves to the venture, and have some inspiration to make the journey.

A lack of clarity in this country about where we are going, what sort of society we are building, has had an unnerving and divisive effect. Some of my own background cannot but contrast the unity that came from a common purpose in time of war, or the confident idealism of the architects of the welfare state – the Beveridges and Tawneys. Where are they now? As the Bible has it in another place: 'Without vision, the people perish.'

We need some spirit to challenge the inevitabilities and fatalisms of our world. The old Welsh preacher, Hugh Pryce Jones, once cried out: 'If anyone says war is inevitable, disease is inevitable, poverty is inevitable, I shout out: "Thank God that's a lie; Jesus Christ lives and his Kingdom will come".'

The four ingredients are all necessary and they balance each other. The caring or family virtues can be soft and sentimental. The stern virtues of discipline and hard work can be stiff and insensitive – as is sometimes the sound of the law and order lobby. Loyalty can be fiercely exclusive and heartless about others. Vision can be mere theory and idle dreaming. I believe that the integrating unity which faith in the love of God gives to such a picture means that a vision of the future is not fudged up by wishful thinking, that discipline has a purpose beyond mere rules and legalism, that loyalties can be passionate but not exclusive, and that the family virtues lose their cloying sentimentality.

To return from ideals to realities. We have committed ourselves in this country to a free society in the belief that this is the right way for society in the end. We cannot, as in Plato's republic and in some past versions of Christianity, act as if there were those who know and they impose their way on others. We also have behind us the achievements of the natural rights philosophy. We have embarked on the way of freedom, of choosing the good through love, in the belief that that is the right way for man in the end. We may fail horribly in the attempt and collapse (as some say the Roman Empire did) in self-seeking, with life all pleasure and no discipline. We *may* rise to using freedom responsibly – to doing things effectively for each other not because of fear but because of fraternity and love.

One thing and one thing alone will decide whether we go up or down and that is the way in which society is quietly affected by those who try to get the better things *caught*, so that they become part of the personality of growing individuals and not something imposed by coercion from outside. It is surely the conviction of St George's, Windsor that Christians should be infectious people in an age of freedom and confusion – but also an age of glorious opportunity.

I have tried in this lecture to look at a vocabulary for justice in terms of human rights. We have seen that its achievements in the past are considerable; but the attempt to elevate that vocabulary into the centre of our moral thinking is a mistake. The pursuit of justice opens out wider horizons. The point about rights is not to stand on them, and the point about justice is to search one's heart before seeking it.

Violence

🖸🖸🖸🖸

THERE HAVE ALWAYS been those who have claimed that they wanted to build a new and better society and they have tried to do it by the way of force and violence.[1] All Christian Churches are agreed that no structure created by violence is stable or good. Means exist in this society for change to occur by peaceful means, by the building of trust and confidence between different groups in the community, but the efforts that have been made in these directions have been gravely hampered by the destruction and the sordid futility of violence. All Christian Churches agree on this. Who can forget the moving words of Pope John Paul II in Drogheda, made all the more poignant now that he has himself fallen victim to a terrorist's bullet? The Pope said:

> I pray with you that the moral sense and Christian conviction of Irish men and women may never become obscured and blunted by the lie of violence, that nobody may ever call murder by any other name than murder, that the spiral of violence may never be given the distinction of unavoidable logic or necessary retaliation.

Who can dissent from the conclusion of the joint Roman Catholic/Irish Council of Churches Working Party on Violence, whose report urges 'that the Churches jointly remind their members that they have a *prima facie* moral obligation to support the currently constituted authorities in Ireland against *all* paramilitary powers'? Thank God there are still men and women with the courage to put their own lives at risk by defending the community and the possibilities of peaceful change and evolution by serving in the police force and the judiciary and all sections of the public services.

[1] Sermon at a service for the consecration of the north transept of St Anne's Cathedral, Belfast, 2 June 1981

Violence succeeds only in breeding violence and brings about a degeneration in the moral character of those who live by it. Some spokesmen for the 'hooded men' seem to speak as if violence were some kind of scalpel, to be wielded by a surgeon in an operation to cut out what they regard as the diseased part of society and to return the body to health. In reality, the instrument, the scalpel, is diseased itself. It spreads infection throughout the body and infects those who take it up.

In the eye of the storm created by men of violence, you have continued to build in a way that I am convinced will endure. Why is this? So much of the tragically misapplied passion has come from bad myths, one-sided ways of looking at the past, which exaggerate the faults and atrocities of the other side and place a halo of romance around the martyrs for one's own point of view. Every nation and every community need a healthy vision and good myths which help them to understand where they have come from and what they stand for. In place of the bad myths of a romanticized and tendentious way of looking at history – and we have all been guilty of this – the Christian Church, of whatever designation, has the privilege of holding up the vision of perfect manhood and of God's love, which came to us in the person, in the life, the death and resurrection, of Jesus Christ. In the words of the Lesson: 'Let each take care how he builds. There can be no other foundation beyond that which is already laid, I mean Jesus Christ himself.' Jesus Christ is the only foundation for a building and a peace which will endure. All other visions must be measured and judged by the love shown by Jesus Christ – his love of his fellow men which went beyond the idols of race or nation and which embraced all without distinction, Jew and Greek, slave and free. The fears and inherited – but false – stereotypes that we tend to have of one another can be broken down by mutual prayer and a determination to build our lives and our conduct on no other foundation but that of Jesus Christ.

Even the violence itself can assist this process. It would be dreadful to sentimentalize the suffering which so many have had to endure as a result of the troubles, but I have been astonished and moved by so many stories in which tragedy has produced clearer vision and a determination to build Christian love and forgiveness, because any other response to tragedy is simply colluding with the hostility to life and to love which lies at the root of violence. I have been particularly moved in the last few days, reading a new book by Alf McCreary called *Profiles of Hope*. Over and over again, ordinary people are revealed as extraordinary in their determination to turn their personal suffering into a constructive contribution to the healing of old wounds and the building of new hope. I was very impressed by the story of the woman who founded the Cross Group, where relations of those who have been murdered meet across the divisions of the community.

One phrase in particular sticks in my mind which was used by both a Protestant mother and a Catholic mother. They said that they were thankful that they were not the mothers of their sons' murderers. 'It must be dreadful to be the mother or the wife of someone who has done something terrible, that really is a harder cross to bear. You can lose someone and still love them but if my son had been guilty of terrorism in any way I would like to think that I would still love him. But it would be terrible to think that a child of mine had treated another human being in that way.' The people in *Profiles of Hope* do not conceal their natural grief under some false veneer of religious assurance. They admit often that they had come close to losing their faith. But in the end they come across as people equipped to understand more deeply the hard way of Jesus Christ and build a better future upon this foundation.

This cathedral is a sign of the patient Christian work that is going on in the eye of the storm. Some may be cast down and even cynical, because things seem not to improve but even to worsen. Some are tempted to lose hope. But one thing is clear: defeatism ensures defeat. Doing nothing colludes with the enemies of life and love and of the faith of our Lord Jesus Christ. There is no alternative to patient, small-scale, local and personal attempts to bridge the divide and to build a new community in a shared love for Jesus Christ. The vocation of all Christians is to be bridge-builders. Here since 1899 in this cathedral you have been patiently building bridges between man and

God and between the different sections of the community.

I remember some years ago, far from here, I was standing by the latest-built big bridge in the world. It was in Istanbul and it joined Europe to Asia. It seemed to join the past to the present: on one side the bazaars and shanty dwellings and on the other the high-rise flats and the Mercedes cars. It was built by a consortium of several nations and across its span passed people of every race and tongue. It seemed a great symbol of hope. Then I noticed that every fifty yards there was a guard. There had been so many threats to blow up the bridge from those who seemed to hate the idea of the human race growing to be one family. It was indeed a powerful image of the modern world, a world divided between the bridge-builders and the bridge-breakers.

Nothing is more important than that the Church today should be found on the side of the bridge-builders. It is at the heart of our faith. Jesus Christ built a bridge between God and man, thus giving a human face to vague ideas of the divine. Inspired by his Spirit, we are called to build bridges between Christians, for divisions between Christians have always cost lives and betrayed the gospel. We are, too, to be bridge-builders within the community in which we are set, because Jesus Christ is not just Lord of the Church: we claim that he is also Lord of all.

One of the most ancient titles of a chief bishop is *pontifex*, bridge-builder, and so I come here simply to preach that gospel and to congratulate you on your building, because I know that you have built not just in stones but in Christian lives as well and that you are building on the only foundation, which is Jesus Christ our Lord, to whom, with the Father and the Holy Spirit, we now offer thanks and praise. Amen.

The Role of Great Britain in Europe

🔲🔲🔲🔲

SOME OF MY predecessors as archbishops of Canterbury have played a significant part in the story of Britain's connection with Europe[1] and none more so than the very first archbishop, St Augustine, who arrived on the shores of what is now my diocese in East Kent in 597. It must be said that he came somewhat reluctantly. The historian Bede records that, passing through Gaul, Augustine and his party were 'paralysed with terror. They began to contemplate returning home rather than going to a barbarous, fierce and unbelieving nation whose language they did not even understand.' Pope Gregory the Great, however, was proof against their pleas and sent them on. Britain had, of course, been part of the Roman Empire, but after the legions left in the early fifth century a series of barbarian invasions wrenched it into a north European orbit and links with the Mediterranean world became very tenuous.

The Church which Augustine helped to build in England was perhaps the chief agent in reintegrating our island into the most sophisticated contemporary western European culture – the Christian culture, which looked to Rome for inspiration and leadership. Britain had come in from the barbarous margin and had entered into a dependence, warmly affectionate at times, on the Roman see. English missionaries like Wilfrid, Boniface, Willibald and Willibrod played a crucial part in extending the influence of the Roman Church and culture into the Low Countries and Germany. A little later, English monks like Alcuin of York made a major contribution to the Carolingian Renaissance and the court culture of Charlemagne.

The Scandinavian invasions of the ninth and tenth centuries had a disastrous effect on the Church of England. Many monasteries, the centres of sophisticated European

---

[1] Address at the Palais des Congrès, Brussels, 4 November 1981

culture and learning, were destroyed and relations between England and the Continent were disrupted. There was a possibility that Britain would become part of the Scandinavian world. Some of my predecessors suffered in the process. In 1012, the Danes murdered Archbishop Alphege. Having failed to extract a ransom for his release, they pounded him to death with mutton bones during a drunken feast at Greenwich.

The Norman Conquest of 1066, however, settled the matter once and for all. Britain's future was firmly linked to that of France and the Continent and the island was penetrated as never before by continental styles of art and architecture and by the French language, which remained the tongue of the upper classes until well into the fourteenth century, and which has left an indelible impression on our own vernacular.

The career of the most intellectual of the archbishops of Canterbury, St Anselm, illustrates this new intimacy between England and Latin culture. Anselm was born into the gentry of north Italy. He became a monk in the abbey of Bec in Normandy and while there he developed the ontological argument for the existence of God. In this argument, which is not without influence even on contemporary philosophy, Anselm maintained that if we mean by using the word 'God', 'than which nothing greater can be conceived', then we cannot conceive of this entity except as existing. He also made a very substantial contribution to the theology of the atonement in his greatest book, *Cur Deus Homo*. This cosmopolitan character was consecrated Archbishop of Canterbury in 1093 and continued to be a significant intellectual influence throughout the Latin-speaking culture shared by the greater part of what we now call Europe.

The mobility which this shared culture made possible is well illustrated by the career of the only English pope, Nicholas Breakspear. When I was Bishop of St Albans, we decided to build a new chapter house next door to the cathedral on the site of a medieval chapter house of the great Benedictine abbey of St Albans. During the course of the necessary excavations, we unearthed several skeletons which we were able to identify with the assistance of a medieval guide to the burials in the chapter house. One of the skulls belonged to Robert the Chamberer, father of Nicholas Breakspear. He has now been reverently reinterred before the high altar of the cathedral.

The story is that his son wanted to be a monk at St Albans, but failed the entrance examination and went to study instead in France where he became abbot of the small Augustinian monastery of St Rufus near Avignon in 1137. He travelled to Rome on monastic business and attracted the attention of Pope Eugenius III, who used him as a papal diplomat. His most important assignment was a mission to Scandinavia, where he reorganized the Churches of Norway and Sweden and made Trondheim into an independent archbishopric. In 1154, he was unanimously elected Pope and, I am glad to say, forgave St Albans for its earlier rebuff and showered privileges upon the monastery, which was named the premier abbey of England.

I told that story at some length to illustrate the extraordinary unity of European culture in the twelfth century, which permitted a lad of obscure family in southern England to pursue an international career, culminating in the papacy.

After the changes and convulsions of the sixteenth century until the time of our own Pope, John Paul II, the idea of a non-Italian pontiff became difficult to conceive. The unity of European culture became more fragmented. Latin gradually ceased to be the lingua franca with the development of vernacular languages and the culture no longer produced Lombards like Anselm, who became Archbishops of Canterbury, nor Englishmen like Breakspear, who became a Bishop of Rome.

In religious terms, the English Church, sundered from Rome in the sixteenth century, developed independently of the continental Protestant Churches. There were those, to be sure, who wanted the Church of England to be conformed to the most advanced Protestant Churches of Germany and Switzerland, but my own predecessor, Matthew Parker, Elizabeth I's archbishop, played an important part in putting the accent on continuity with the native English tradition. His most considerable work was, significantly, entitled *The Antiquities of the British Church*. The development of a self-consciously English church tradition in the following century which looked neither to Rome nor Geneva for final authority naturally had the effect of further reducing the ease of cultural commerce and traffic between England and the Continent.

This development, however, did not lead the Anglican Fathers whom I most revere to arrogate to themselves the name of the one true Church to the exclusion of all others. The declaration which all priests still have to make before assuming any office in the Church of England begins with the phrase, 'The Church of England is *part* of the one, Holy, Catholic and Apostolic Church'. The best Anglicans have never tried to pretend that all wisdom is concentrated in our own island, but they have acknowledged and cherished the virtues of the Churches of the Continent.

Sir Thomas Browne speaks for this tradition. He was an Anglican layman of the seventeenth century, who had received a doctorate at Leyden and practised medicine in the city of Norwich. In his greatest work, *Religio Medici*, he expresses his loyalty to the Anglican tradition: 'I am of that reformed, new-cast religion wherein I dislike nothing but the name; of the same belief, Our Saviour taught, the Apostles disseminated, the Fathers authorised and the Martyrs confirmed.' But his loyalties do not blind him to the virtues of other Churches, nor lead him to deny the name of Christian to those who differed from him in doctrine and among whom he lived during his time in the Low Countries:

> There is between us one common name and appellation, one faith and necessary body of principles common to us both; and therefore I am not scrupulous to converse and live with them, to enter their churches in defect of ours and either pray with them or for them ... At a solemn procession, I have wept abundantly while my consorts, blind with opposition and prejudice, have fallen into an excess of scorn and laughter.

The best of the English Anglican chaplaincies in Europe, which began to be founded in the reign of Elizabeth I, are of this tradition. Proselytizing is inappropriate. Chaplaincies were established to serve the English abroad and their descendants, and not to poach on the preserves of other national Churches but to promote that reconciliation which Sir Thomas Browne desired when the 'revolution of

time and the mercies of God' may permit. I am proud to
have been an English chaplain abroad myself and to have
spent my honeymoon as the chaplain in Nice.

There is, of course, a ruder tradition which is, alas, more
notorious and not entirely played out, even in our own day
– the Little Englanders' traditional isolation. I was looking
at the accounts of some of those who had come this way
before me – English travellers to the Low Countries – and I
came across some choice pieces of invective, written by the
nineteenth-century poet, Robert Southey. Where Sir
Thomas Browne had said: 'I could never hear the Ave Mary
bell without an elevation', Southey, writing from near
Liège in 1815, remarked: 'The church bells were very loud,
frequent and troublesome – this annoyance alone would
have told us that we were in a Catholic country.' At the
same place, he confided to his journal that 'they brought us
grapes and Gruyère cheese at breakfast. The butter was
marked with the IHS – a mark of devotion, I believe, not the
initials of the vendor.'

In this modest historical survey, I have tried to escape
from generalities by looking at the relations between
Britain and Europe in an ecclesiastical perspective, using
illustrations some of which, I hope, have been unfamiliar to
you. In order to avoid misunderstanding I must confesss
that I have not done justice to the 'Great Britain' of the title
and have omitted the equally complex and fascinating
stories of Scottish, Irish and Welsh relations with Europe,
but I have been anxious to spare you from cultural
indigestion. I have tried instead to sketch the development
of a shared European culture, have glanced at its fragmentation and at two of the characteristic attitudes which the
English have adopted towards their European cousins.
What of today . . . ?

It is undeniable that there is still confusion in Britain
about where its loyalties and future lie. Dean Acheson's
judgement that Britain has lost an empire and not yet
found a role remains to a large extent true. Little
Englanders still exist who believe that all would be well if
we withdrew from foreign entanglements, but the complexity and interdependence of economic and political life
in the modern world make isolation an impossible option. It

is also I believe undesirable, since any Christian who believes in the Fatherhood of God must respect the brotherhood of man and recognize that obligations and responsibilities to neighbours go far beyond any political divisions or national frontiers.

Another strand of British thinking sees our loyalties and our future lying in association with the British Commonwealth and we would certainly not wish to surrender the links we have. The personal friendships and the understanding which come from being members of a worldwide Commonwealth are of particular significance as we consider what best can be done to assist the development of the Third World. The Anglican Communion of which the Church of England is a part is more than ever a worldwide Church in which black members are a majority. Much of the Anglican future lies in Africa. It is perhaps symbolic of the change in the balance of influence within the Christian Churches as a whole, that my first and very happy meeting with the Pope took place not in Europe but in Accra, the capital of Ghana.

As well as ties with the Commonwealth, many people in Britain cherish a sense of kinship with the United States. Hundreds of thousands of American troops have died in Europe. Marshall Aid helped to reconstruct the Continent after the war and for the past thirty years or more the relative peace which Europe has enjoyed has relied heavily on friendship and alliance with the Americans. It would be foolish for any of us to forget these things but I do not believe that they should be seen as substitutes for the European vision.

The Treaty of Rome was itself an act of reconciliation, and had a vision of a peaceful and prosperous united Europe. It was to be a rebirth after half a century of ruinous conflict and waste of European energies. But if birth is a desperate business, rebirth is even more so and certainly in Britain there were doubts and hesitation which held us back. A Belgian, Paul-Henri Spaak, was one of the visionaries and original architects of a reborn Europe and he made every effort to persuade us to participate in the venture when it began. He was bitterly disappointed when his arguments failed. But when we did finally join the

Community Belgian leaders helped ease the way and welcomed our arrival.

The European Community has already achieved much. War between member states is already unthinkable. There has been a real attempt to tackle some of the major technological and economic problems too big for any individual nation state to solve by itself. But it is still undeniable that in Britain at least the European Community has a communications difficulty in expressing its underlying vision in a sufficiently vivid and generous way. Failure in this respect could be very damaging. It is obviously going to be hard to make progress if there is no vision of where we are going sufficiently strong to harness the energies which are easily diverted into mutual suspicion and the selfish kinds of nationalism.

As the Pope said of the European future, 'The institutions alone will never create Europe'. The institutions are essential and it is no part of my intention to make cheap points about the bureaucrats of Brussels, many of whom are idealists themselves. But I believe that all of us involved in the rebuilding of a better Europe have a responsibility to articulate a clearer vision of the kind of society we are working to create. I want to suggest three key words for that vision – reconciliation, compassion, meaning. I want to suggest also that, just as the Church inspired and defined the old Europe, so Christians today have the potential if only they have the will to make a decisive contribution to the new Europe.

Reconciliation

We must never forget Eastern Europe. Whatever the nature of our divisions, the countries of the East remain culturally and historically part of Europe. We have that basic reason to work for our present reconciliation, but in addition, in an age of nuclear weapons our present divisions could well prove fatal. The Iron Curtain is not a totally insurmountable barrier and our aim must be to re-establish that freedom of travel and mobility of ideas which was possible in medieval Christian Europe.

There has to be an end to name-calling and mutual

abuse. We have to learn once more to listen to one another and to continue talking in order to uncover our contrasting assumptions and to improve our chances of understanding and having sympathy with each other's problems. The Christian faith shared by so many in Eastern as well as Western Europe is a good basis on which to build this kind of reconciliation. There are vigorous Protestant churches in East Germany. There is the indomitable Roman Catholic Church of Poland and there is the Russian Orthodox Church in the Soviet Union. Most of my own experience has been in this latter area and over some years of contact I have made many friends. Christians in these countries want very much to be in touch with the West and we should make every effort to build on their willingness. It is not possible to be a follower of Jesus Christ and to be negligent about the search for peace and reconciliation.

At present there are two specific Christian attempts being made to bridge the divide. Both Archbishop Sundby of the Lutheran Church of Sweden and Patriarch Pimen of Moscow have been working to organize peace conferences next year when the special United Nations' session on disarmament will be held. I intend to support both these initiatives. Although all through history governments have tried to manipulate the Churches, I do not think that we ought to be cynical about the possibility that these conferences could contribute to the building of the trust and confidence which will be needed if we are to make progress step by step with the East in mutually reducing our armaments to a lower and lower level. One day I hope that it may be possible to organize a world religious summit for peace in some neutral place and this question ought to be on the agenda of the meetings to be held next year.

Belgium is a good place for a Christian leader to talk about reconciliation as a keyword in a vision for Europe. In a special service on All Souls' Day, I was privileged to celebrate the Eucharist in the Mercier chapel of Malines Cathedral and to recall in prayer on that occasion all those who took part in the Malines Conversations. Those Conversations were held in the 1920s in an atmosphere vastly different from that of today. Then there was a divide of suspicion and even hostility between Roman Catholics and Anglicans which was bridged by comparatively few. Cardinal Mercier was such a bridge-builder and his courage and hospitality have borne astonishing fruit in friendship and mutual respect between the Roman Catholic Church of Belgium and the Church of England. Most recently Archbishop Daneels and I have discovered one another to be united in similar hopes and problems. We have become friends and I take away some very happy memories from my stay in his house.

Anglicans hitherto have been less a part of the new current of church life and thought on the Continent but now we are making more effort, thank God, to listen to the ideas of our closest neighbours in Europe as well as maintaining the already deep and lively links with the Church in places like Central Africa. If Europe is to become more and more a community of the spirit, better communication between the Churches can make a vital contribution to the process. Cardinal Mercier took a risk for the sake of reconciliation and gives us a good example.

On a recent visit to Dublin I saw a further vivid illustration of the creative possibilities of taking a Cardinal Mercier-like risk. In St Patrick's Cathedral, the door of the old chapter house has a hole in it. In one of the feuds between the Ormonds and Kildares in fifteenth-century Ireland, the Kildares had chased some of the Ormond clan into the chapter house and besieged them there. After some days the Earl of Kildare began to think that it was monstrous for men of the same faith to be feuding on holy ground, so he offered a truce. The Ormonds were too suspicious to accept or to open the door, so a hole was bored through it and Kildare thrust his arm through to the other side. After some moments it was clasped in friendship and the door was opened. That was the origin of the English phrase 'chancing your arm' and in the cause of reconciliation within the community and with the East, Christians ought to be chancing their arms like Cardinal Mercier.

Compassion

A healthy and human person is compassionate and societies without this element shrivel up. It should be obvious that you cannot build any kind of community if you are always harping on your own individual and sectional interests. There are people within our own European Community, the handicapped, the unemployed and the old who need support but there are also the unimaginably poor in the hunger belts of Asia and Africa who have a claim on our fellow feeling and compassion.

The nations of Europe have left their mark in the furthest corners of the world: we spread our ideas and profited from the trade which expansion brought us. The European influence has been seminal and we must now channel it into constructive compassion for poorer nations. The Lome Conventions established principles which have greatly benefited the Third World but I believe that the Churches can play a role in mobilizing popular enthusiasm for aid and development policies. In Britain our efforts are partly inspired by the energy and success achieved by the Churches of the Low Countries in alerting the public conscience to the need for these policies. This could not be more important at the moment as we wait to see whether the positive communiqué from the Cancun Summit is able to generate more will to turn the vision of the Brandt Commission's programme for survival into concrete policies and action. There is little time to waste. If you picture the world as a great ocean liner, then most of Europe is sitting in the first-class dining rooms. Unfortunately, water is pouring into the steerage where the poorer passengers are huddled. The captain and the crew must take some time from devising ever more sophisticated menus for the first-class passengers in order to deal with this threat to the whole ship. My hope for the Churches of Europe is that they will not be found saying grace in the first-class compartment as the ship sinks, but will be trying to raise the alarm. If we fail with the problems of the steerage we shall not remain insulated from the effects of the incoming water for ever.

It is too easy to be cynical about the reserves of altruism which exist in our European societies and the capacity of people to rise to a moral challenge. While in the United States I had lunch with Robert MacNamara at the World Bank. He told me that he had been to the Harvard Business

School to talk about the Brandt Report. He had begun by
passing over the moral arguments on the assumption that
his audience would be more easily convinced by arguments
from self-interest and the interdependent character of the
world economy. Afterwards he was taken to task for his
omission and the students of the Harvard Business School
began a vigorous discussion of the moral ideas behind
Brandt.

Meaning

I believe, however, that there will be no energy or will for
reconciliation or compassion if there is no positive response
to the crisis about the meaning, purpose and value of
human life, which is evident in all our European societies. If
people come to be engulfed by cynicism and the conviction
that their existence is meaningless and futile then very
little positive good will be able to flourish in such thin soil.

For us Europeans, these questions are being posed
particularly sharply as we see the old patterns of work and
employment giving way before profound economic and
technological change. The forms of work generated by the
first Industrial Revolution have given a structure and a
value to millions of lives in Europe but what will happen if,
for example, manual labour becomes less and less necessary
both in mechanized agriculture and in the new silicone chip
industrial culture? Some people in England are still talking
about a return to full employment but now it is probably
more realistic, as well as helping the casualties of change,
to develop new attitudes for the time which seems to be
coming when working for a living will not potentially
occupy the best part of a lifetime. This could be a creative
development.

The Christian Church has never valued human beings
for their productive capacity or for their salary-earning
potential. We believe that in the last analysis human beings
were created for no functional reason but for delight, to
love and be loved by God their Creator. It is hard to see this
in the world as it has become, a world in which some people
have to bear more than their share of squalor and misery.
We must work hard to relieve their suffering but must not

forget in the process what the end result, the fully human society, is supposed to look like. We have been rather too busy for delight and wonder these last 200 years but now we are being re-educated by a revolution of the times. Now is the time to see again that the arts that express delight, and the cultivation of a readiness to comprehend wonder, are not luxury items for our fragmentary leisure hours. They are close to the heart of a human life that has meaning and fulfilment. I find the words of the English poet Robert Browning very inspiring:

> This world's no blot or blank,
> It means intensely and means good:
> To find its meaning is my meat and drink.

Without a vision the people perish. I believe that Europe needs a generous vision if it is to flourish, one that puts the accent on reconciliation, on compassion and on the search for meaning. That kind of vision is, I believe, capable of overcoming some of the natural rivalries that remain and would certainly enhance Great Britain's contribution to the Community. I also believe that the Churches have much to offer in all these areas but only if they are prepared to think, search and act in conjunction with other men and women of goodwill, who may not be able to share the Christian faith. A Church trumpeting its certainties while circumstances are changing may rally some of the fearful but it will just as surely cause even deeper and more bitter divisions within the society it is seeking to serve. Churchmen are not exempt from looking for the new things which God is teaching us through new conditions of life and work. We must seek to cultivate a non-exclusive confidence that although the future is full of uncertainties, the author of the process is God and he is its guiding spirit. This kind of confidence can set us free from the fear which is immobilizing some of the best in our societies, free to be reconcilers and men and women of active compassion. It is a kind of confidence that reduces the need to resort to uncreative dogmatism which denies a place in Europe and a share in its future to anything or anyone that is not Christian. It is a kind of confidence that can save the Church from retreating into a sterile antiquarian ghetto.

The Church and its teaching once played a vital role in giving Europe unity and identity. I believe that the united Christian community has the potential to be a vital catalyst in the rebirth of a European community of the spirit. This short visit has already made me more determined than ever to work to make this vision a reality.

A Proper Patriotism

🔲🔲🔲🔲

IT WAS ON a Sunday in September, forty years ago, that the decisive engagements of the Battle of Britain took place.[1] We are here to remember those events, to honour the courage of those who fought for the mastery of the skies above our country and to give thanks for the sacrifice of those who gave their lives or were terribly injured in resisting the invader.

Nowadays, people are inclined to be cynical about heroism or embarrassed by it but I am not ashamed to use the word 'heroic' about many of the people who took part in the Battle of Britain, not only those in the air but also ground-crews which suffered their own, heavy toll of casualties. Very many of those I should want to mention by name are here, so I shall spare your blushes and simply reflect on the fact that the Battle of Britain revealed extraordinary qualities in a great variety of people, many of whom looked quite ordinary in civilian life.

Some of those who were involved in the battle from Biggin Hill were very young – nineteen, or even younger. Even wing commanders were often only twenty-five and group captains not much older. Others who flew from this airfield were not even British citizens. It was an international force with the brave Poles, Free French and, later in the War, volunteer Americans of the Eagle Squadron as well as recruits from the Commonwealth countries, all playing their part in the battle. One of the most dangerous fashions of our time is the tendency to belittle human beings and to reduce them to the lowest common denominator of greed and self-interest and to deny the element of altruism and even heroism in the human character. It is dangerous because, if you can sneer at heroes, you can convince yourself that everyone is nearly always out for

[1] Address at the Battle of Britain service, Biggin Hill, 21 September 1980

himself. I give thanks for the heroism displayed in 1940 as an antidote to this kind of denigration.

I also give thanks unashamedly for the *victory*. Hitlerism did represent a threat to the values on which our country has been built and the experience of the Church in Germany revealed the profound hostility of Nazism and Christianity. None can doubt that the RAF played a vital part in preserving these islands from an alien and oppressive tyranny. Yet wars do not in themselves solve the deepest problems of human life: at best, they give us a breathing-space in which we can build and work for a world in which war will seem an obscene irrelevance. An American admiral said: 'The function of force is to give time for moral ideas to take root.'

To give thanks for heroism and for the victory achieved in 1940 is not to glorify war. As a soldier, I saw something of the war in Normandy and Germany; you saw much more here at Biggin Hill. Combatants are only rarely the ones who are tempted to glorify a war which involved so much pain and loss. The victory of the Battle of Britain purchased, at great cost in human lives, 'time for moral ideas to take root.'

The best tribute we can pay to those who fought in 1940 is to work hard to insist upon and establish some of the values taught by the Christian faith and partly shared by other men of integrity and goodwill. To illustrate what I mean, I would like to recall a conversation in the book by Richard Hillary, *The Last Enemy*. It was a book that had a profound effect on me in 1942; the other day, I read it again.

Richard Hillary describes a railway journey in the company of his friend, Peter. They are the young bright fighter pilots of 1940. Richard claims that the war means to him above all an opportunity to grow faster, to explore the limits of his own personality, a road to self-fulfilment, and he prods the normally inarticulate Peter into a statement of the ideals for which he was fighting. Men of action are properly suspicious of rhetoric or bombast but, if ideals are not from time to time articulated, they wither in the silence. Having listened to Peter's creed, Richard replies: 'You are an anachronism. In an age when to love one's country is vulgar, to love God archaic and to love mankind sentimental, you do all three.' Peter is killed in the Battle of Britain but his example and influence continue to grow inside Richard, particularly when he is horribly burned and blinded. I want to suggest that Richard's caricature of Peter's position contains unfashionable truths still worth serving and planting into our present world.

'Love your country.' It is vulgar, said Richard Hillary. We might say that it is worse than that. After all, in fighting against Hitler we were fighting against an ideology which pushed love of country to the point of idolatry. Love of country always needs to be balanced by love of our neighbours in other lands and needs to be submitted to the test of the love of God. But I would say that love of your country is essential to any healthy society. Our local loyalties for a squadron, a regiment and a country are nurseries for our affections. Of course they need to expand in scope but it is important that we do not combine a theoretical love for people in distant parts with an inability to get on with our family or the neighbour next door. Our love for our own people equips us to respect and sympathize with the love other people have for their countries. If you cannot love the brother you have seen, how much reality is there in the love for the brother you have not seen? Love your country: correct what is amiss with her, but with gentleness born of respect and affection.

'Love God.' Richard, at one stage in his life, called this 'archaic'. Certainly, if religion becomes just mouthing antique language, a matter only of nostalgia and formal piety, it is useless, but I believe that the picture of what the world was meant to be, and the full stature of man, cannot be seen without experiencing and practising the love of God. The love of God rescues us from the self-obsession which Richard Hillary found so imprisoning. It draws out the best qualities in us which remain buried if we live locked-up, selfish lives and it gives us the confidence to act and to hope at a time when so many are afflicted with an immobilizing sense of fear and futility.

In 1940 the odds seemed overwhelming and similarly now for many the problems seem so complex and the dangers of nuclear war and of violence fuelled by hunger and despair so close that their will to act and work is sapped. Love for God and trust in him gives us not a shallow optimism about the immediate future but the hope to continue to work and struggle for a better world. 'Find your strength in the Lord' said our Second Lesson. Love God and 'you will be able to stand your ground when things are at their worst, to complete every task and still to stand'.

'Love mankind.' Richard Hillary called it sentimental, and of course it can be. The person who is much exercised by causes far from home and ignores need on his doorstep is not unknown but the love of God which delivers us from selfishness also pushes us out into a love of the world beyond our door, a world which is just as much God's creation as our own familiar landscape. The love of mankind, however, cannot be left in the realm of entertaining warm feelings. The potential for violence in the world is terrible and immense. Unless we use the time our force has bought us to turn our love into aid and development programmes for the poor and hungry then our children may have to face conflict on a scale and of a ferocity that could not be imagined in 1940.

Love your country. Love God. Love mankind. Each one of these commands by itself contains great dangers. Love of country without love of God or mankind can turn us into rabble-rousing chauvinists. The love of God which does not overflow into love of our neighbour is arid and sterile. The love of mankind without the hope born of faith in God can bring us close to despair as we reflect on the sorry history of this century and what man has inflicted upon man. Together, love of country, God and mankind compose a vision which is worth working for and struggling for. This vision is never an anachronism, as Richard Hillary discovered. Our best tribute to those who fought in 1940 to win us space and time to plant the moral ideas which will grow into a world that is more just and loving is to work hard to give this vision substance in family, in school, at work and among our friends.

Love your country. Love God. Love mankind.

The Church and the Bomb

🔳🔳🔳🔳

IN THE COURSE of this debate on nuclear weapons and
Christian conscience,[1] a large area of ground common to all
Christians has already been mapped out. Full-scale nuclear
war would be incalculably disastrous for our world. It may
be possible to enter a just war in which gains will be in
proportion to inevitable damage, but there can be no such
thing as just mutual obliteration.

Christians can never have an easy conscience about
nuclear weapons. We must interpret the signs correctly.
The cloud illustrated on the cover of the Report represents
the outcome of man's attempt over hundreds of years to
manage, to dominate his environment and to impose
himself upon nature and his fellows. Ironically, the effort
to achieve mastery has brought us to a point where we
have unbound unmanageable forces. The cloud is a
judgement on centuries of aggressive intention. In such a
dangerous situation, the Church, in particular, has a
responsibility to speak with great care. That means at least
an assault on hygienic words which promote complacency
and on the propaganda and distortion which increase hostility between the peoples of the world. Action on these two
fronts can change the climate in which decisions are made.
Respect for the word, intellectual, moral and spiritual,
is the first step in maturity, said Dag Hammarskjöld.

The working party's report is exemplary in this respect. I
would like to add my voice to the tributes already paid to
the Bishop of Salisbury and his team. They have not fudged
the truth that when we are talking of a world in which so
much human talent and so many scarce natural resources
are being wasted in the production of weapons of mass
destruction, we are talking about a world that is in the grip
of madness.

[1] Address to General Synod, 10 February 1983

So far I would be surprised if there was very much disagreement. But now we come to the crucial question. How do we get from where we all know we are to where we all want to be? We cannot disinvent nuclear weapons and they are a clear sign that we live in a world which is in rebellion against its own interests – a world which has rejected the order given to it by its Creator. How do Christians fulfil their vocation and prime moral duty to be peacemakers in such a world? I regret to say that I do not find the recommendations contained in *The Church and the Bomb*, and further amplified in the Bishop of Salisbury's amendment, entirely coherent or convincing. I do not believe that unilateral measures of the kind suggested will in fact have the effect 'of getting multilateral reductions moving.'

Now we are all seeking to achieve arms reductions and to stabilize the balance of terror at a lower level of armament on both sides. This must be done in negotiations, as section (c) of the amendment suggests, but my fear is that the kind of action being advocated will actually undermine the negotiations now in progress in Geneva. There are good reasons for believing that, faced with mounting internal economic and social difficulties, the leaders of the Soviet Union are seriously committed to the success of the present round of negotiation. It would be a tragedy if the Soviet will to make progress, for example in eliminating the most threatening weapons in Europe, were to be weakened by the spectacle of the NATO alliance in disarray and the tempting prospect of gaining great diplomatic advantage by consolidating a nuclear as well as a conventional superiority in Europe.

Too often this country has appeared to send misleading signals to those who have been tempted to pursue aggression. Make no mistake, an announcement of the 'United Kingdom's intention[2] of carrying out, in consultation with its allies, a phased disengagement of the United Kingdom from active association with any form of nuclear weaponry' would have a traumatic effect on the NATO

---

[2] The Bishop of Salisbury's amendment in these terms was defeated (100 votes for, 338 against). The Bishop of Birmingham's amendment, calling for Britain and her allies to 'maintain adequate forces to deter aggressors' but to 'forswear the first use of nuclear weapons', was accepted (275 votes for, 222 against).

alliance. I have seen very little evidence that those responsible for policy in other NATO countries would regard renunciation of nuclear weapons as anything other than a repudiation of the cornerstone of NATO's defence policy. On the contrary, I have heard much to suggest that such a step would put a new strain on the alliance on which the peace and stability of Europe has rested since the Second World War, by strengthening the advocates of isolationism in the United States.

My worries about this are not just on grounds of prudence and credibility. The basis of alliance is a willingness to share responsibilities. Is there not some moral inconsistency in seeking to remain within an alliance which accepts a policy of nuclear deterrence while declining to take one's share in the means by which that policy is sustained?

Another understandable but, I fear, forlorn hope expressed both in the Report and in the Bishop of Salisbury's amendment, is that Britain's gesture might have an exemplary effect and do something to halt the proliferation of nuclear weapons. The Report says that the United Kingdom should renounce its independent deterrent 'in the hope of putting new life into the Non-Proliferation Treaty'. In fact, there are now 119 parties to the 1968 Non-Proliferation Treaty, which is the largest number of countries adhering to any current international agreement. The principal non-signatories of the Treaty are concerned much more about regional situations (Argentina and Brazil or India and Pakistan) than they are about the general attitude of the nuclear powers. It is most improbable that a unilateral gesture by the United Kingdom would bring in any new signatory. Recent experience suggests that no country wishes to incur the international odium of flouting the Non-Proliferation Treaty by openly declaring itself a new nuclear-weapon state. India, for example, when it exploded a nuclear device, maintained it was for peaceful purposes only and that country has been very careful to uphold this position and has thereby demonstrated that the Non-Proliferation Treaty does have some bite. Since I believe that the unilateralist approach would undermine disarmament negotiations in progress without exerting much exemplary influence, I cannot accept unilateralism as the best expression of a Christian's prime moral duty to be a peacemaker.

I emphatically believe, however, that we cannot be satisfied with the present *status quo*. There is a deep-felt longing in Western Europe to see results from the negotiations which are now taking place in Geneva, and a feeling of urgency about the need to reduce the level of nuclear armaments on both sides. That is natural and right, and I would associate myself with the conviction expressed by the Pope that 'in current conditions "deterrence" based on balance' may still be judged morally acceptable, 'certainly not as an end in itself but as a step on the way towards a progressive disarmament'.

This is a moment to seek not only to stabilize the balance of terror, but to gain fresh determination to build more effective international institutions to ensure common security. I think that we should be paying more attention to the plea of the new Secretary-General of the United Nations, Señor Perez de Cuellar. He describes what he calls 'the new international anarchy' and lists some steps which governments ought urgently to consider: greater use of the United Nations mediation facilities; more immediate resort to the Security Council; and the building up of the United Nations' policing capability. The Secretary-General is talking about the provision of arrangements for the world which are possessed by the humblest local authority – an ambulance, a fire brigade, a police force. It is strange that the subject is so neglected in comparison with disarmament.

A new world order is not, of course, only a matter of a more efficient police force. We should not forget the contention of the Brandt Commission that the denial of justice to the hungry and poor in the world will have more and more explosive consequences. There are so many barriers to our sympathy and compassion; so many stereotypes of one another that make talk of brotherhood merely theoretical. The Pope's New Year message emphasized the importance of a commitment to 'dialogue' as a way of reducing dangerous misunderstandings and tensions. In theological conversations with Russian churchmen and through many personal friendships with ordinary people in the Soviet Union, I have come to glimpse the differences between our mental furniture and basic categories of thought. It seems worse than ironic that we are running down Russian studies in our schools and universities just at a time when we are increasing our defence spending.

But peace is not just something for high-powered dialogue or international commissions. We have to acknowledge that the springs of violence and war are in everybody. This is implied in the UNESCO constitution: 'since wars begin in the minds of men, it is in the minds of men that the defences of peace must be constructed'. To embark on this involves a profound and costly personal repentance, and sometimes even peace groups, who have done so much to dent our complacency, can manifest the kind of unrepentant and unreflective aggression they so readily ascribe to others.

Someone said to me about this debate that it is really a debate between faith and principle on the unilateralist side and pragmatism on the side of the multilateralists. I do not believe that that is true. I do not impugn the honesty or good faith of those who support unilateralism, but I believe there is also moral seriousness in the multilateral approach. It is a prime moral responsibility, I repeat, of a Christian and it is the strategy which our Lord commended, to build peace in an immoral world. The way of negotiations and building new international institutions also demands moral courage and perseverance.

Principle is not the exclusive possession of those who are attracted to larger gestures. Our Church takes pride in the achievements of Wilberforce and Shaftesbury, who in the last century helped to bring to an end the slave trade and the brutalizing of children. We sometimes forget that their vision had to be translated into relentless pegging away at detailed facts. Principle also belongs to those whose moral sense expresses itself in the painstaking precision and care about detail which I have found among some of those actually involved in disarmament negotiations. I hope that this Synod will be united in signalling to them our understanding, our respect and our support.

Ambassadors for the Prince of Peace

🖻🖻🖻🖻

I SHALL REMEMBER 1981 as the year of the peace marchers.[1] All over Europe, all kinds of people have joined together in massive demonstrations for peace. This is understandable. It is a dangerous world. If a war did start in Europe, even one fought with so-called 'conventional' weapons, it would be of unparalleled destructiveness. Millions of ordinary people showed this year that they were not satisfied with the priority being given by their leaders to the search for peace. We seem to have made depressingly little progress in building up trust and confidence between nations and the impatience of the peace marchers is right.

They are also right to be especially anxious about the huge arsenals of nuclear weapons being assembled by both East and West. The only conceivable justification for possessing such vast power for destruction is that it gives us a breathing-space in which we can try to build the kind of relations between East and West that have made war between ancient enemies like France and Germany unthinkable. Better understanding is very hard to achieve when you are dealing with a political system which does not permit its citizens to travel freely and controls the flow of information, but there is no excuse for doing nothing to build bridges over the divide. The peace movement this year has kept up the pressure on our own leaders in the West. It has, I believe, succeeded in strengthening the will and determination of those at the top to make progress in the search for peace.

You may not think that this is a very Christmassy theme for an archbishop to choose, but of course peace is a major theme of the Christmas story. 'Glory to God in the highest and on earth peace, goodwill towards men', sang the angels. Jesus himself was hailed as the Prince of Peace and he said

[1] Article in the *News of the World*, 20 December 1981

to his followers: 'Blessed are the peacemakers, for they shall be called the children of God.' Any Christians worthy of the name have to be peacemakers and of course many individuals are members of various peace movements, but I am often asked, 'Why isn't the Church doing anything?'

The Church is, in fact, doing a great deal. Did you know that the World Council of Churches has just completed a hearing in Amsterdam on nuclear weapons? This meeting brought together experts and Church leaders from the USA and the USSR, as well as many European states. Did you know that in May next year the head of the Russian Orthodox Church is to be host to a worldwide peace conference in Moscow, of religious workers for peace? Did you know that, after the United Nations' special session on disarmament next summer, the Scandinavian Churches, led by the Swedish Archbishop of Uppsala, are to hold an international Christian peace conference?

Of course, politicians sometimes try to manipulate the Christian Churches for their own ends, but British Christians should not fail to support these initiatives. We should be there to help ensure that these conferences do not just add to the combustible state of the world by dealing in accusation and indignation. I hope that these gatherings might allow people to listen to unfamiliar points of view with the kind of tolerance and respect which leads to understanding.

The Christian Church exists in both East and West. Some of the most vigorous Christian life is to be found behind the Iron Curtain and in the so-called Third World. I know that from my personal experience of Christian friendship in Poland, which is so much in our thoughts and prayers today, and I know it from visits to strong and growing Christian Churches in Africa and Asia. A shared belief in Christ provides the basis for the unity and trust which is not thwarted by political frontiers or different languages.

But you do not create peace simply by preventing war. Conflict exists in the world because of human selfishness. People act as if they were the centre of the world and everyone and everything else existed for their benefit. If you are always harping on your own rights and ignoring the rights of others, then you rapidly collide with them. Some of the loneliest people I know are often found in comfortable surroundings, busily attempting to build the world entirely around themselves.

Jesus Christ, the Prince of Peace, comes to unite us all to the true centre of life. Peace and the harmony God intends for the world depend on our coming to see and know God as our Father. But he is not only a Father for us; other people are also his children and therefore our brothers and sisters.

We are being hypocritical if we claim to be supporters of peace and do nothing about our own attitudes to other people. Peace is not only a matter of the Foreign Secretary travelling between capital cities. Certainly, we ought to keep up the pressure to see that this work is done, but we must also be determined peacemakers in our own relation- ships in the family and at work. If we can rid ourselves of violent thoughts and contemptuous ways of talking and looking at other people and become a point of stillness, then peace will radiate from us like ripples on a pond. An old Russian saint summed it up when he said that the man with peace in his own heart could convert the countryside for 200 miles around. I am convinced that he was right and that we need not despair, even when faced with the big issues of peace and war. To do nothing about demonstrating for peace, or making peace in our own family circle, is the kind of defeatism which ensures defeat.

This Christmas, I hope and pray that you and all those you love may know the peace which this world cannot give, the peace which was brought by the Christ Child.

ASPECTS OF EXPERIENCE

🔲🔲🔲🔲

The Waste Land

🔲🔲🔲🔲

YOU ARE BEGINNING the celebrations of your anniversary year[1] in Advent. Nature is in a dark mood and it is dark, too, for many individuals and for the culture and country of which we are a part. We have devoted ourselves to exploring and mastering outer space, to dominating and organizing our environment. But there is a tragic contrast between our achievements in outer space and our failures in inner space, the world inside us, the world of our hopes and experiences, where there is much poverty, shallowness and confusion.

In particular, we must face the truth that in these inner spaces it is exceptional for modern men and women to have a really vivid experience of the presence of God. In past ages, whatever blemishes there were and whatever failures there were in outer space, this experience of God was widespread. In the Bible, there is no attempt to prove God's existence. His existence was obvious and the Bible is addressed to the question of what response is appropriate. But now God's existence is not obvious or even plausible for many of our contemporaries. Even among Christians there are many honest and courageous people who can only lay claim to a flickering communion with the light and a fleeting and intermittent experience of God. Instead, there exists in the inner spaces a waste land. T. S. Eliot's poem of 1922 is still prophetic. We find ourselves in the Waste Land:

> A heap of broken images, where the sun beats,
> And the dead tree gives no shelter, the cricket no relief,
> And the dry stone no sound of water.

This waste land is trackless: there are no clearly marked

---

[1] Sermon preached on the inauguration of the 850th anniversary of the diocese of Carlisle, Kendal Parish Church, 3 December 1982

paths in such arid and rocky country. Here in the inner space which is the proper birthplace and home of the light, you find people wandering directionless and lost.

Oppressed by the glare, people understandably seek ways out. They try to fight a sense of futility and soothe the pain that comes when life has no meaning by a flight into narcotics or drink or too much food. I vividly remember a student saying to me when I tried to remonstrate with him about his excessive dependence on real ale: 'Drunk or sober, it is all a road to nowhere.' But this way of living solves no problems; rather, it creates more debris and broken-down human beings. It is one of the ways in which the waste land grows.

Other would-be escapers act as if the rock-strewn landscape could be made green and fertile again by the kind of human ingenuity, effort and technique which have conquered outer space. They ignore the fact that the rules and logic of this inner world are entirely different. We even see this in the Church. There is a good deal of managerial 'busyness' about. The Church has needed reform at all stages of its history. It is, of course, good to manage our necessary affairs efficiently but nationally we have broken out into a rash of interdepartmental memos, working parties and conferences; a hail of paper descends and leadership becomes choked with an indigestible volume of information and initiative. Paralysis by analysis! The shady trees are turned into paper, which becomes litter, which feeds the waste land. Activism of this kind often springs from anxiety about the aridity of the inner spaces and contributes to their dryness by producing exhaustion. Every church body, every diocese, particularly in Advent, particularly in its 850th anniversary year, ought to scrutinize its meetings and activities very closely to achieve reductions.

Another pseudo way out, which is, alas, only an escape into a blind alley, is the manufacture of spiritual excitements. Particularly in the early stages of the Christian life we are given spiritual sweets to encourage us: feelings of exultation and peace, experiences of transfiguration, to nerve us for the inevitable difficulties ahead. These are precious gifts from God and we give thanks for them. But there is a temptation to manufacture counterfeits when God for some reason has withdrawn his sweets. Everywhere you meet attempts to manufacture some hectic community exuberance to give us warmth and comfort. This is very understandable and it even has an amusing side to it. When I was visiting the United States, I was told about a church in New York which ran a very popular evening Communion service. When the moment came for the peace to be exchanged, they turned the lights off for twenty minutes. But fizz is not faith and it is not lasting. Eventually the bubble bursts, leaving further weariness in its wake to feed the waste land.

This is a time for giving thanks for what we have received, for taking stock and for being sober and honest about where we stand now. We do this in the confidence that Jesus Christ is our living stone, the cornerstone of the great achievements of the Christian past, but also the shadow of a great rock in a weary land under whose shade we can pause and look at the truth unafraid. He also teaches us that 'Whoever remains in me, with me in him, bears fruit in plenty; for cut off from me you can do nothing'.

He teaches us that new life and light in the inner spaces are given to those who have learned to look, listen and receive. No man has ascended to heaven; no man has stormed heaven; we must put ourselves in the posture to receive the living sap that comes only when we are rooted in Jesus Christ. The techniques appropriate to outer space – management and manufacture – techniques not to be despised for their capacity to transform our world, do not work in the inner spaces and only add further debris to the wilderness.

I hope that in your year of celebrations there will be much exuberance and excitement, fireworks and theatricals; but I hope also that there will be renewed emphasis on a serious study of Scripture, time for teaching about prayer and, even more important, time for prayer. I also hope that there will be more urgency about pondering the teaching of the Christian Fathers and the theological tradition of our own Church, as we strive for greater clarity in our presentation of Christian teaching about God and eternal life. I am convinced that the Church will only make its full contribution to debate and action about social issues when it is firmly in touch with a living tradition with some theological cutting edge. Promiscuous benevolence is not enough. 'Whoever remains in me, with me in him, bears fruit in plenty; for cut off from me you can do nothing.'

Jesus himself was driven into the waste land for forty days after his baptism and he was also offered some false ways out. Most significant of all was the Devil's offer of power over the kingdoms of the world. Jesus was tempted to import the way of management from the world of outer space and apply it to the building of the spiritual kingdom. The living stone and our shadow of a great rock in a weary land resisted the temptation and instead waited in the waste land, poring over the word of God in the Scriptures and, by fasting, setting himself free to hear and receive. It was then that the angels came and ministered to him. Jesus persevered in the desert, and just as manna came to our forefathers there, so for Jesus the wilderness became a fruitful field, a field of true vision and light. Like the sword, Excalibur, which in the Arthurian myth rose from the lake, the true vision comes from beyond ourselves. It is given, not grasped. If we are cut off from Jesus we can do nothing. That is one of the unfashionable and derided truths we stand for as Christians. It enables us to look, unafraid and with brutal realism, upon the waste land and not be consumed by it or driven to despair as we wait under the shadow of our great rock, Jesus.

The vision and the light which are the gifts of God are not problem-solving formulas that have eluded the wise down the ages. They are gifts to those who have learned to be still and to be expectant, to listen and to receive the created word of a new birth into God's own life. This new birth fills us with the sap from the one true vine. It brings us the capacity to see and to love with the eyes and the heart of Jesus. The presence and activity of that new life in the Church is the power which makes the desert of the inner spaces fruitful again.

Fellowship in the Gospel

I GREET YOU all as brothers and sisters in the name of the Lord Jesus Christ.[1] We may look different. We may speak different languages. We may wear different clothes. But we worship the same God and we believe in Jesus Christ as Lord and Saviour. That is the most important thing about us all. I give thanks that he has brought us together today. I give thanks that he is known and followed by so many in this country.

I am a new archbishop, This is my first journey out of England since I was made archbishop at a service in Canterbury when Archbishop Bezaleri and Archbishop Wani were present. They supported me and now I come to support them, for these are days when all Christians must support and learn from each other if we are to help build a better world.

Your new archbishop is a personal friend of mine: I ordained him a priest in England. He has often spoken to us there of his love for his people, and the gifts which I have brought have been made by many Christian friends. But over the years he has brought me greater gifts: stories of the faith, of the courage and love of those of you who are building a new church here on the same foundation that the old church is built on in my country. We share what St Paul called a *fellowship in the Gospel*. Wherever we meet to do any new thing for Jesus Christ, we can say that the Lord is here, his Spirit is with us.

Now, as on the day of my enthronement in Canterbury Cathedral, so here, in very different circumstances, we rejoice that it is in his presence and in his strength we undertake every new venture, and I give you a text from our common Bible:

[1] Sermon at Bukaru, Eastern Zaire, 11 May 1980

But ye shall receive power, after that the Holy Ghost is come upon you: and ye shall be witnesses unto me both in Jerusalem, and in all Judaea, and in Samaria, and unto the uttermost parts of the earth. And when he had spoken these things, while they beheld, he was taken up; and a cloud received him out of their sight.

I suppose many of you here will be farmers. A good number of you at least will have your own gardens, and grow your own crops. You will know how important the heavens are to the farmer. A wise farmer will look there with some care. When, in the distance, he sees the first clouds, he knows they speak of change. Soon, the sun will give way to rain and the thirsty earth may be made ready for planting. A wise farmer will tend the earth with care. The soil which he feels beneath his feet will only feed him if he digs, plants and waits. A wise farmer looks to the heavens for the blessing of rain and for the life-giving power of the sun. For his part, he and his family must do all they can to make the earth ready. They must be good stewards. If the farmer did not have simple faith that the sun would rise and that one day the rains would fall, he would neglect the earth and soon his family would suffer and die.

It is not too difficult for farmers and for those who live close to the land to understand the message of Jesus. The message of Jesus is 'good news', good news that the great Creator, God, is a loving God who, through his Son, walked this earth and out of love died that we might live. He rose from the dead and ascended into heaven. Those who are called Christians and follow Jesus are baptized with water and receive the blessing of new life. Just like the farmer, they are called to have faith and to play their part fully and responsibly. Just as the farmer prepares the soil, so must the Christian constantly tend his soul. As he does this, in company with his brothers and sisters in the Church, so he is able to be open to the blessings of God and new life will grow and flourish.

Today, when a new province of the Anglican Communion is being created and a new archbishop enthroned, we first of all look to Jesus who ascended into heaven having won the battle against sin and evil. Like good farmers, we prepare to turn our hands to work and to the preparation

of the ground so that the Holy Spirit of God may continue
to work in all fullness. How can we prepare and continue to
plant?

Many years ago, a young Jewish man scratched the
following message on to the wall of a ghetto:

> I believe in the sun, even if it does not shine;
> I believe in love, even if I do not feel it;
> I believe in God, even if I do not see him.

Today, when we are all together from so many different
places, it is not too difficult to have faith and to feel the
nearness of God. Soon, this day of rejoicing will pass and to
each and every one of us will come the day and time of
testing, the day when we cannot see the sun, when the
rains do not fall, when we feel and experience hate and
when God seems far away. It is during such days that faith
takes on a new meaning; it is during such days that we
really need the fellowship of the Church, both within and
beyond the borders of this new province.

When a new province is made, we are not creating a
separate lake or pool. A pool, when the waters are still, will
soon turn dark and stagnant. When a new province is
made, in one sense the Christians of that province join a
river. They put themselves alongside Christians throughout the world, and together they move forward towards
the Kingdom of God. At quiet points along the river, there
are pools which are still and deep, but they are constantly
refreshed by new waters. At other points, the river surges
along with tremendous energy and life. The different
moods and expressions are all part of the one river, the one
Church throughout the world. The river of the Church of
God fertilizes more of the world than its people sometimes
suppose. Members of that Church are made members by
baptism and by faith. As we are called to live in faith, so
some may be called to die for their faith. If the river spreads
too thinly over the land, it soon loses energy. In the heat of
the day, when the sun is high, the river will be in danger of
drying up completely. All rivers need a certain depth, and
all rivers need quiet pools. That is another way of saying
that the province must base its life on prayer and worship.
It is the prayer of Christians which gives depth to the life of

the Church. Leaders in the province will encourage this by their own lives and example.

As the river has banks to stop water spilling over the land, so the Church, the community of baptized believers, has simple boundaries. All members enjoy life together in the family of God and, after preparation, share together in the great family celebration, the Lord's Supper, or, as it is often called, the Eucharist or Thanksgiving. This family occasion is a time when together we can enjoy the fruits of faith, and when we may share and be renewed by the very life of Christ himself. We should note carefully that such sharing in the life of Christ is always also a sharing of life with each other in a community. Our life in Christ is deeply bound up with our life together, for 'we are members together of the one body of Christ'.

Within the context of a living, praying, worshipping, witnessing community, God will call us for special tasks. First, there will be the recognition by all that they share in a common vocation to follow our Lord and to be living witnesses to him wherever they may be. Second, there will be those who grow to recognize that they have a certain call to the ordained ministry of the Church. Those who recognize this call will first of all recognize that this is a call to service, to serve the whole people of God that the whole Church may grow to be faithful to its vocation. Just as the whole Church needs to be constantly educated in Christian understanding, so those who are called to the ordained ministry of the Church will need specialized theological education. It is always a mistake to be less than thorough in providing good foundations. 'Thorough preparation for mature partnership' might be one of your mottoes. Partnership between archbishop, bishops, clergy and laity, the partnership of brothers, not the kingdom of rulers. Partnership between dioceses, the partnership of equals in Christ, not the superiority of nations. Partnership between nationals and non-nationals: the partnership where differences of colour or tribe do not divide but mutually enrich. Partnership in mission: the partnership of mature and responsible participation together in the work committed to the whole Church.

It is not part of our mission as Christians to tempt

members of other Christian communions to join our own Anglican Communion. It is always part of our mission to proclaim by word and deed faith in our Lord Jesus Christ. This is a faith which demands a simple yet profound loyalty: the loyalty to Jesus and his Church.

Mission will flow from a healthy faith and belief in Jesus, and in trusting to the power of the Holy Spirit. We do not engage in mission simply to build up the Church and to increase numbers. Of course we look for individuals to be added and we receive them with joy, but mission in part points to the Kingdom of God and speaks of the kingdom of justice and truth. The Church, as the body of Christ here on earth, is called to stand on the side of justice and truth, and may be called to pay a heavy price for this, as our brothers and sisters in Uganda have experienced during recent years. To say this is not to encourage reckless or foolish action. It is to say that the Church must always have a special concern for the poor, the oppressed, the victims of injustice and those who have no voice. Deep pools, where proper discernment may take place, are certainly needed if this ministry is to be lived in fullness.

When Archbishop Luwum died, a missionary had a dream. He dreamed that he was standing in Africa. In the distance, he saw a fire. As he approached, he saw that in the midst of the fire was an African, but he was not being burned, and he heard a voice which asked him to place his own hand in the fire. Not all Christians are called to be martyred for the sake of their faith, but all are called to touch the living fire of the Holy Spirit, and to be touched by that fire.

The wise Christian, like the wise farmer, will look to the heavens with some care and with some discernment. He will prepare the land with some effort, and in the name of Christ will allow himself to grow towards wholeness in growing harmony with earth, heaven and his fellow men. May God bless this new province. May God bless your new archbishop. May God bless each and every one of you. May you grow in the strength and in the maturity of the Lord. In love, we welcome this new province to the Anglican Communion. We ask you to accept us as we are. Together, let us look to heaven where Christ reigns on high;

together, let us tend the earth, that we may work for the kingdom of justice, truth and peace. Together, let us link our hands around the world, that in the fellowship of our faith we may be faithful witnesses and servants to the one who ascended into heaven, who sits at the right hand of God the Father Almighty, and will come again in glory to judge both the quick and the dead.

The Christ-Like Life

🔲🔲🔲🔲

SOMETIMES IN THE past we have over-identified Christianity with its western cultural trappings.[1] The gospel arrived with an English face and came to be associated with surpliced choirs and the Ancient and Modern hymn book. Christianity had the appearance of a foreign religion. There was hardly another strategy open to the early missionaries if they were not to sink without trace, and we should take care not to adopt an attitude of lofty superiority to them. Those who worshipped in the matshed church on the parade ground where now the Hong Kong Hilton stands, and those who built the Cathedral of St John were often men and women of energy and self-sacrifice. But that period is over. The Lord's name is to be great among *all the nations* and here in the East where the sun rises, the Lord should have a Chinese face.

The face of the Christ Child seen by the wise men at the first Epiphany was obviously not an English face, but it has been a fundamental Anglican principle that every nation should praise the Lord in its own language and draw on its own cultural traditions. The three-self movement was known in the Anglican Church in the sixteenth century when the Reformers determined to have the Bible read and heard in English. They devised a liturgy in the language of the people and they established a Church which, while not abandoning Catholic doctrine, had local autonomy and self-government.

The time has come in the life of the Church here to be more thoroughgoing in the application of our principle. There should always be some provision for worship in English, but Christ must come to have more of an authentic Chinese face. If his name is to be great among all nations, Christ's connection with the resonances and

---

[1] Sermon in St John's Cathedral, Hong Kong, on the Feast of the Epiphany, 1982

achievements of one of the oldest and most venerable civilizations on earth must be made clearer. There should be no excuse to repeat the old slur: 'one Christian more, one Chinese less'. This will take hard work both in the realm of social action and service to the community and also in the Church's life of worship. I hope that there will be efforts to develop a liturgy more thoroughly rooted in the Chinese cultural tradition, particularly as it is expressed in music and drama.

We must, however, face the difficulty at this point. Too much identification with any particular national culture could be a betrayal of the Christian gospel. The Christ Child at the first Epiphany was firmly rooted in the culture of Israel. The gospel of St Matthew begins with a great roll call of his Israelite ancestors. But Christ also scandalized the Jews. He made revolutionary demands and claims. His life and teaching judged the culture of his own time. If Christianity is no longer an irritant, if it no longer seems fresh or excessive, if it simply becomes a bland hobby of a few cultured people, then it has clearly failed.

One of the most fashionable words in the Church at the moment is a rather ugly one: indigenization. It stands for a very good principle, and one that has been fundamental to the Anglican Church, that Christ should come to have the face of every nation under the sun. But clearly we also have to ask the question: What are the universal truths behind the local faces? If being a Christian means that we wish to grow into the life of Jesus Christ and become people who see with his eyes and work with his hands, then how do we know that we are actually on the road to becoming like Christ the Son of God and not just taking an easy, undemanding, familiar way?

Our Church believes in local autonomy, but it also values as indispensable the existence of a worldwide family of fellow pilgrims united around certain essential Christian values. I find these values in the Bible, and in particular I wish to suggest that the holy Scriptures give three marks of authentic Christ-like life which of course have to be translated into local terms, but which hold good for all times and all places, for the first Epiphany and for this one. I find those marks in the words which Jesus said when he shared the Last Supper with his disciples. You remember that he took bread with thanksgiving. He broke the bread and gave it to his disciples. Those are, I believe, the three marks of a truly Christ-like life which should characterize individual Christians and the Church in all times and in all places: taken with thanksgiving, broken, given away.

Taken with thanksgiving: this was a fundamental attitude of our Lord. Even in the night that he was betrayed, he gave thanks. Cultivating the practice of giving thanks is not just a way of paying a debt to our Creator, it helps us to see and receive life in a different way. If we spend our lives demanding our rights and in self-assertion, then we become clenched-up personalities and hard characters. As we are more and more filled with thanksgiving to God for food, for our friends and families, then we open out into people who are aware of life as God's gift, and we become sensitive to the divine love at the centre of creation. If we are growing into a thankful Church, then we know that we are on the road to becoming more Christ-like. The Church in Hong Kong has been given many privileges and opportunities, and every act of worship ought to include some note of thanksgiving.

Jesus Christ did not assert his rights. He emptied himself and was content to take the form of a servant. His open and loving attitude to other people made him vulnerable. He suffered and was broken. That is the second mark of a Christ-like life. When I was in Burma recently, I met the former Archbishop, Francis Am Ya. I was humbled by his modest references to the occupation of Burma during the Second World War and by his account of his sufferings in prison. He said that he was very grateful for those experiences, painful as they were, because they had helped him to mature as a Christian. The Christian gives thanks for his own sufferings and brokenness, not in a spirit of masochism, but because, for Christian believers, suffering can spotlight and dislodge our obsession with ourselves, and make us fit for the service of others.

Being broken prepares the way for the third of the marks of an authentic Christian life, self-giving. At the Last Supper, Christ said: 'This is my body, this is my blood.' He gave himself to us in the most profound way. He put himself at our disposal. A broken man is a man who has created the possibility of rebuilding his life around Christ. Only when Christ directs your hands, when he looks with his compassion through your eyes, will the deepest self-giving become a reality.

I have been moved and impressed by examples of your Church's service to the community in Hong Kong. I have seen the activity and practical compassion at St Thomas' Church Centre, and I have also visited St Christopher's Children's Home. I was particularly moved by the Michael Temple Cottage. That cottage was founded after the painful death of a six-year-old child, and that suffering has been turned into a caring and happy home of other six-year-olds. The Anglican Church here has, I believe, shown by its deeds that it is not only interested in the privileged, and this is the way in which I pray church life will grow here.

Life taken with thanksgiving and brokenness leading on to self-giving: this is the faith which we must indigenize. This was the light seen at the first Epiphany and in the life of our Lord Jesus Christ. This is the light which we must kindle for the sake of the world now.

Christmas

🄶🄶🄶🄶

I USE AN old-fashioned version of the gospel but I wish you, with all the enthusiasm of today, a very happy Christmas.[1] 'Glory to God in the highest and on earth peace, goodwill towards men.'

Christmas should be a time of celebration and encouragement. But even on the first Christmas Day we find the shepherds 'sore afraid'. Ever since, Christmas has been both a time of comfort and a centre of controversy. In 1652 Parliament was presented with a 'terrible remonstrance against Christmas Day'. This led the House of Commons to order the abolition of the festival and to resolve to meet on Christmas Day itself. We do not find ourselves now at such a moment of crisis but, talking to people this year, I find three attitudes to this festival which could pull us apart rather than unite us more deeply. There is the man with the child in his eyes. There is the man who has left behind childish things. There is the man with pain in his mind. I believe that there is truth in each of these attitudes and that they need and correct one another.

The man with the child in his eyes is the person who cherishes the traditional Christmas virtues. He puts the emphasis on the simple things which have not changed for thousands of years: motherhood, family affection, friendship. We all realize how much we depend on the love of others. When God speaks through a child, he speaks a most human language.

Among my Christmas cards I treasure one from a distinguished scientist which has this quotation: 'The enlightened man regards himself as an adult who can no longer allow himself the pleasure of repeating stories that so delighted his childish age. But this is an oversimplified picture. We might well ask whether childhood has not its

---

[1] Sermon in Canterbury Cathedral, Christmas Day, 1982

own special values – a happy trustfulness, a particular candour, which the grown man should preserve at all costs unless he is to land in dogmatism or sterile cynicism.'

We all recognize the dogmatic man who knows all the answers because he has not faced most of the questions. We find him neither convincing nor attractive. We all recognize the cynic who does not believe or trust in anything or anyone and we find him the least reliable of men. But those who retain in maturity a simple trust in God and a candour and openness with people, we recognize, respect and love. They are the ones who are at home in Bethlehem, for of such is the Kingdom of God.

But this childlike vision in maturity is not the same as childishness. The man who has put behind him childish things also has his place in the stable. Many people whom I meet think that they have rejected the Christian faith because they can no longer accept what they were taught at primary school. People who have developed emotionally and intellectually cannot be satisfied with a picturesque stable full of charming and sanitary animals. A chocolate-box religious understanding shrivels up as we face the suffering which comes even to the most fortunate in this world.

We have sentimentalized the Bible and the man who has left behind childish things can help us to see the brutal realism of Bethlehem. Joseph and Mary are displaced persons. They move from their home in obedience to an edict – the word is *dogma* in Greek – from a government which is organizing a census, treating people as numbers. St Luke includes this detail to point the contrast between the wonder and tenderness of God's gift in the birth of a child and the demands of the system imposed by emperors, government officials and high priests. The birth itself is quickly followed by the massacre of the Holy Innocents – another terrible picture of the clash of compassion and a mother's feelings with *realpolitik*. The Christian hope was born in the darkness and the light of Christ continues to shine in the darkness which is acknowledged but which has never conquered.

The man who has put away childish things can help the Church to make contact with the man with pain in his mind. He is the serious type who reminds us that our rejoicing must not make us deaf to the cries of misery of the world.

This Christmas, who could forget the parents of Richard Dewes, the boy from Sutton Courtenay who was murdered a few days ago? This can be a cruel and violent world in which we hear 'Rachael weeping for her children'. Our hearts go out to all victims of violence and all those who love them. Then, as we sing the angels' song, 'peace, goodwill to all men', the world faces terrible danger. Some of our best minds and a large proportion of our precious resources are employed in preparing for the lunatic unthinkable. Full-scale nuclear war is unwinnable and there should be an end to all talk which makes it seem anything other than madness.

I sympathize with those who have a pain in the mind and will not let the subject drop. I applaud those who demonstrate for peace, but the protests and gestures are not enough. In a world of conflicts, where human beings still resort too easily to force as the quickest solution, we must spend at least as much energy supporting and improving the international links and organizations that already exist to help us grow into world citizens. In a world where the consequences of failure are deadly, we must develop more effective international authorities capable of adjudicating and composing quarrels when they arise.

Jesus Christ came with a message for all mankind regardless of sex, creed or class. There is also a place in the stable for those who are determined to stand up for that and to fight for a universal order in the world. This is a way to hold back the chaos which our selfishness threatens to unleash upon all human kind. The scale of this operation would seem to be beyond us, but little Bethlehem reminds us that it is not the size of the effort but its intensity which counts.

Let us lay off indignation this Christmas. Stop blaming, judging, carping and condemning one another. This is a day for pooling our resources. We need the man with the child in his eyes, in alliance with the man who has left childish things behind him, to give hope and courage to the man with pain in his mind. They are all at home in the stable and all needed if Christ's coming is to have an impact on our world in 1983.

Here is a prayer which I hope you will all be able to say in the midst of your celebrations today:

> Father of all mankind, deepen our gratitude, enlarge our sympathies and order our affections in generous and unselfish lives. In the name of Jesus Christ, your Son, our Lord, who is born today and who lives forever to draw all mankind to your love. Amen.

The Blessing of the Oil

🔲🔲🔲🔲

MANY CUSTOMS ARE associated with Maundy Thursday.[1] The name of the day comes from the Latin word *mandatum*, which means commandment. This is the day of the new commandment 'that you love one another'. Most of us think of the Last Supper, the Eucharist, the sign of our communion with the Lord of Love and with each other; or perhaps the feet-washing, the sign of loving service in the name of Christ.

On this day there is another ancient custom, the Blessing of the Oil, a sign of the healing ministry of the Church. We have good news for human ills, and so also attached to this custom is the tradition of priests gathering round their bishops as a sign that we are at one in this ministry. 'Behold how good and joyful a thing it is to dwell together in unity. It is like the oil' – oil of healing, oil of harmony. The symbolism of oil in the ministry is a very simple one. Oil is a medicine, an emollient. It soothes what is sore, softens what is stiff, moistens what is dry. This is the kind of healing Christ can bring to his people, banishing soreness, stiffness and dryness of body and spirit.

Throughout the Orthodox and Roman Catholic world there is always a special celebration of the Eucharist on this day, to express joy in the healing which comes from God, to express our unity in the Sacraments which are a sign and vehicle of this ministry. In the Armenian Church all the oil that is used all over the world in the Armenian communities has been blessed at the holy place of Etchmiadzin in Soviet Armenia. It is a sign of the unity of this ancient Christian people. I have been to Etchmiadzin in Holy Week. On the first day they collect the herbs. On the second day they make the oil, on the third day of Holy Week they boil the oil and on Thursday they bless the oil. Now that we have an

[1] Sermon in Canterbury Cathedral at the Liturgy of the Blessing of the Oil, Maundy Thursday, 1981

Order for the Blessing of the Oil, I thought we would bring this small ceremony out into the open and arrange a service in the cathedral at a time when the clergy, as well as some of the laity, are free.

Of course you will have domestic celebrations in the parishes this evening, but this is a day when by tradition it is possible to take Communion for a second time. It means that at the heart of the diocese in Holy Week we are giving thanks that all healing flows from God and for the sacramental signs of that healing. It means that we shall be praying for the sick in body, mind and spirit. It means that we can give thanks for our priesthood and pray for the unity of our ministry together. It is also an opportunity to pray for those who celebrate the Easter mysteries, that they may be fortified and directed aright.

Often in the course of a year diocesan administration may seem distant, impersonal and remote. Archbishops and bishops seem authority figures, far removed from the cares and concerns of ordinary priests in the ordinary parish or from the chaplains in the hospital. Here is a chance to share as brethren together at the simplest level in what our work is all about. We share in the gospel and we share in the Sacraments which bring that gospel into the present.

Two thoughts about Sacraments have influenced me greatly. The first is in a book by Oliver Quick on the Sacraments. He said that Sacraments represent a truth of the gospel, and that they are also instrumental in helping to achieve that truth. So, for example, God is someone who wills our healing. When we anoint someone, we not only represent and declare that truth but we also change the situation. I would that this custom of anointing to declare and to assist might be more commonly used. Sacraments are real but they are not magic.

Then there is a quotation from Father Kelly, the founder of Kelham, in which he was trying to defend the objectivity of Sacraments against the heresy that their actions depend upon our degree of worthiness. He wrote:

> The position I am trying to explain can only be expressed in the words, *I want Christ*. And I mean that just in the sense of a child crying in the night, *I want Mother*.

We grown ups may believe, and the child may learn, that although Mother has gone away, she is not far off; but we shall not persuade ourselves and we shall not persuade the child's trenchant truthfulness that this is the same thing. It is enough for me, and more than I deserve, that I may find my Lord at all – if, however, I am told that even that initial fact depends on any capacity of my own, depends in any degree on my spiritual state or force – this, may God help me, I will not believe.

It is hard for me to make any response to Christ, to find the energy to worship him, or the faith to believe in him when he does come. If I am to find the energy and faith to fetch him I must give it up.

That is all enough to justify our Maundy Thursday service of the oil.

Remember above all that this is the day of the Lord's giving. We may reject his gifts; we may distort or evade his gifts; but they are always generously available to us. He gives the new commandment, he gives the Eucharist. He gives our partnership in the ministry of the gospel and Sacraments. In all this the Lord wills our wholeness, our unity as priests and as Christian people.

Behold how good and joyful a thing it is, brethren, to dwell together in unity. It is like the oil.

The Cross

◫◫◫◫

FOR NEARLY TWO thousand years the cross[1] has cast its shadow over the world. So on this day of all days where should we meet but by the cross? But where should an archbishop start in talking to you about the cross on Good Friday? Perhaps with the one that I wear nearly every day whether I am dressed up for special occasions, or off duty and informal.

It was designed for me by a young artist, someone of about nineteen, who was herself searching for faith. It seems to me in what she said that she found a good deal, because when she gave it to me on the day I was made bishop she said:

> I want to make something plain and simple, not fancy or fussy or merely decorative; a kind of chunky thing that I might wear round my neck at a party, because the faith for which you should stand is one that ought to speak to ordinary people in a real world and not be a bit of icing on top of a cake. It ought to be all of a piece with your own life.
>
> I also want it to be strong, made out of true metal, so that you can grasp it in the demands and difficulties of your work, whether it's an awkward meeting or a difficult interview, because we all need faith to draw strength for daily living.
>
> But I'm going to make it look different from different angles, give it a kind of mobility. I can't, I'm afraid, hang a mobile round your neck and I don't want to be gimmicky, but I want to make this point, that faith does say different things to different people at different times. For the young it has to do with adventure; for the elderly, serenity and consolation; for the people who are up against it, courage and bravery.
>
> And then I'd like it to catch the light and reflect it, since faith is something to be shared around.

All those things are in my mind as I try to speak directly and simply with this cross around my neck, so that I can help to

[1] A Meditation for Good Friday, on Thames Television, 1980

strengthen you in faith, recognizing of course that there will be different messages for the variety of circumstances in which we find ourselves and as we try to share together and help each other in this meditation.

At first the cross seems something strange and harsh and there is no doubt that through the centuries there has been an attempt to soften the harshness of it all. That is why it has been gilded and beautified – sometimes it looks as if Christ had been crucified between two candles on an altar rather than on Calvary. But I suppose Christian art and Christian thought have tried sometimes to draw the sting of the cross. It is a symbol of triumph, of course it is that, but it has been turned into a kind of trophy or magical object, and in centuries when the Church was confident and powerful, the suffering seemed excessive and unnecessary.

Perhaps in this century, if we are to be brought up against the original, stark, simple realism of the cross, we could note how, when it comes to honouring sacrifice or heroism, we can find no better way than this simple sign. Across the battlefields of Europe stretch line after line of crosses but sometimes we forget why we can find no better sign than this.

> And they bring him unto the place Golgotha, which is, being interpreted, The place of a skull. And they gave him to drink wine mingled with myrrh: but he received it not.
> And when they had crucified him, they parted his garments, casting lots upon them, what every man should take. And it was the third hour, and they crucified him.

Focusing faith on a cross is like building hope on a gibbet and seeing good news in a hangman's noose, and we must never allow familiarity to blunt the sharp edge of this story. After all, in the beginning Jesus Christ in his teaching and in his ministry encouraged and seemed to pour healing and hope over people. They followed him, but then at the last they forsook him and fled. He was condemned by the forces of law and order and the religious leaders of the day as a common criminal.

If ever there was a failure in worldly terms here it is, and if we have never been tempted to run away from Jesus dying on the cross, then it is very probable that we have never understood what it means. But we are not here to think clever thoughts or to weave complex patterns. We are here to be realistic and to be watchers – watchers around the mystery of the cross for a while together on this Good Friday. Let us pray for strength to be still and to understand.

> Father, there are many roads by which men and women seek for truth: Help us to follow your way, the way of the cross, quietly, honestly and openly so that you may speak to us in our homes, in our minds and in our hearts. Through Jesus Christ our Lord.

So why do we call this Friday Good? Clearly the first disciples did not see it as such. It was an execution and the end of their hopes, and most of us know something of that awful experience when hope goes dead and the bottom is knocked out of life. Though we hope for the best in life, and that is part of the business of being human, those hopes are constantly contradicted and frustrated. After all, each time we open the newspapers we are confronted by some appalling tragedy. Instead of the meaning which people search for, there is pointless waste; instead of communion with our fellows there is isolation; and instead of hope there is so often despair.

> And at the ninth hour Jesus cried with a loud voice saying, Eloi, Eloi, lama sabachthani which is, being interpreted, My God, my God, why hast thou forsaken me?

Why did the execution of Christ give birth to hope and a faith which transformed the world? It was certainly a strange beginning for any faith. Jesus does not promise worldly success. Islam, which has taught me a lot about spiritual clarity and a God-centred world, began with the highly successful career of Mohammed, charged with the word of God, which brough unity to desert tribes. The religion of the Buddha, which has taught me much about serenity and calm, finds its force in detachment and withdrawal from human tragedy.

Christianity is not about successful living or detached calm, but about the triumph of love. The Easter event, the

resurrection, was an event which transformed the demoral-
ized followers of a convicted blasphemer into a world-
converting force. They discovered that Christ was alive,
but this Christ, as Scripture records, still bore the marks of
the cross. For Christians, love wins. It is victorious, not by
force or compulsion, but by love. This means, and this is
most important, that the Easter resurrection is not a
reversal of Good Friday, not a kind of divine abracadabra.
The Christ who lives is the Christ who points us to the
cross and says, 'That is the way of love and love is the only
thing which is truly invincible and eternal'.

The clenched fist is the way in which many people
believe victories are won in this world. But this violent
world of conquering brings retaliation and in turn the
inevitable crushing of the conqueror. By contrast with the
clenched fist, Jesus Christ's way is the open arms and the
open hands. The hands were open to receive the nails of the
cross. The open hands are a great symbol of the Christian
way. Open arms and hands are not good weapons of
aggression, but they draw the world together, and Jesus
Christ, with his arms wide and his hands open, draws men
and women to himself and brings unity, not by the sword
but by accepting love even to the end. It was the sight of
this love that wrung from the centurion, the Roman
soldier standing at the foot of the cross, this judgement,
this first testament, 'Truly here is the Son of God'.

> Oh God, you have shown us in the life and teaching of Jesus
> Christ the way of love. You have also shown us in his
> suffering and his death that the path of love may lead to the
> cross and the reward of faithfulness may be a crown of thorns.
> Help us to learn these hard lessons so that even in the darkest
> hour of trial we may see the shining of an eternal light. Amen.

What does our contemporary world look like if we see it
through eyes and minds marked by the cross? It is so easy
for this all to be distant from us, but you do not have to look
very far among your friends or members of your family to
find people who are locked into this vicious circle of
conflict, or injury and retaliation which it seems no one can
stop. We meet sarcasm with sarcasm, insult with insult, so
violence with violence. It is the same in the political sphere.

Seldom does a week go by without appalling pictures of the troubles in Northern Ireland appearing on television and in the press. Violence breeds violence, and no one seems to know how to stop it. There is a common-sense logic that if someone hits you, you hit them back. But common-sense logic has led to a world in which there seems to be no answer to most of our problems of personal and political conflict. In the light of the cross, the Christian gains courage to follow a different strategy. Like Christ he is to absorb injury at great personal cost and pain. He has even to keep up an active goodwill for the people who have done him harm. 'Father forgive them, for they know not what they do'.

There is a community in Northern Ireland dedicated to this way of forgiving and accepting. It is the Corrymela Community. It looks like a holiday camp and that is what it is. But its sole object is to mix Roman Catholic and Protestant children together. Centuries of hatred and mistrust seem to be rolled back as you see these children on an adventure course. It is part of their holiday but it is a part where they put their lives in each other's hands and stretch out their arms to help each other. It happens to be a community of which I am proud to be a patron and I believe that supportive efforts of this sort can say far more than any words.

> Lord, make me an instrument of your peace.
> Where there is hatred, let me sow love.
> Where there is injury, pardon.
> Where there is doubt, faith.
> Where there is despair, hope.
> Where there is darkness, light.
> Where there is sadness, joy.

It is often said that, surrounded by thousands, you can be lonelier in the big city than anywhere else in the world. That is where you find real isolation and desperation. Violence or vandalism, cynicism and self indulgence are the fruits of community breakdown. I matter, I count – and to hell with the rest of you. The battle for the soul of our own world will be lost, I suspect, or won in the great cities of the world. What is the strategy of the cross in these circumstances? The Christian whose life has been marked by the cross stays in places of dereliction offering not simply programmes of improvement, although those are important and to be fought for, but offering Christ's long-term strategy.

I have been inspired by a movement founded by the Frenchman Charles de Foucauld. It is not a movement that has hit the headlines, but it exists right across the world in many of its great cities. Without parade or histrionics its members settled down to live a community life. They have seen God is there in the city and they breathe upon the embers of their own deep Christian love, a love which comes from a sense of living close to God. They are not so much setting an example, but sticking with those who feel pushed around by the powerful and at the mercy of impersonal forces for their jobs and their future. The cross and the Christian faith do have something to say in the lovelessness of the inner city and suburbs just as they have something to say in a beautiful country church.

> We thank you, Lord, for those who in their thought for others leave no room for pity for themselves, for those whose faith brings light to dark or dreary places and for those whose patience inspires others to hold on. Help us to turn all our days, our strength and our talents into giving, offering, inviting, loving, for the sake of Jesus Christ our Lord.

I could give you many more examples but I want to draw your attention to one last feature of our modern world, namely the hopelessness which is to be found among so many who have so much. In the film *Darling* there is a scene where a politician appeals to an affluent casino audience for funds for charity. The politician's words and the hardened faces of the casino's patrons form a stark contrast:

> Never have I seen so many hearts so obviously in the right place. I am sure I have no need to bring to your attention the plight of our brothers of every creed, race and colour, in every far-flung corner of the earth, who, at this very moment, are suffering the humiliation, degradation, shame, of the agonies of malnutrition.

That is of course a caricature. But there may be something of all of us in it when we let things and possessions matter most. What does the life of a consuming, possessing world look like in the light of the cross? The cross is the reversal of all the values we are most inclined to cherish, where the accent is on consuming and possessing. The values of the cross can be summed up in loosing hold, giving, offering and inviting. The cross is the supreme expression of the truths at the heart of our faith. Those who would give their lives and will lose them, and those who will lose them for the sake of Jesus Christ and his Father will taste and see the life which is forever full of joy and peace. Paradoxically, the answer of the cross to the hopelessness of the consumers and the possessors is losing and giving. Often it is those who have least who have taught me about real joy and generosity. You only need to visit a club for the handicapped and compare the faces with those of the actors in the scene from *Darling* and ponder, who are the handicapped as human beings?

> Thank you, Lord, for the inspiration of those who possess little and give much. Deepen our gratitude, enlarge our sympathies and order our affections so that we may lead generous and unselfish lives.

I have, like most people, a private picture gallery of men and women whom I admire and in whom I have seen something of Christ, the living Christ. They are people of the twentieth century. There is the German pastor Dietrich Bonhoeffer, whose letters from a German concentration camp inspired thousands of Christians to discover how to live with true freedom in the world. There is Archbishop Luwum, who left few words behind but was an example of a Christian leader who refused to be pushed around as a puppet by Amin. He paid for it with his life, but as a result the Church in Uganda has never been stronger. Mother Teresa, caring for the dying in the squalor of Calcutta, keeps alive a vision of human dignity. You never think of Mother Teresa's race, she seems to belong to the world. I believe she is Albanian, the one country that reckons to have stamped out religion altogether. Then Alexander Solzhenitsyn, whose faith brought him suffering. A tough sort of compassion comes through that face. And Martin Luther King, who had a dream of a world where all men and women were brothers and sisters.

But this meditation is not about notables. It is about all of us who call ourselves Christian. If we are to have a faith which is genuine and strong for all seasons and circumstances and is something which can be shared across all the frontiers of life, it must be big enough for the sort of world in which we have to live, a world of mystery and complexity. But it must be personal enough to speak to each one of us as an individual. None of us can find that kind of faith, ultimate security, rest and a deep lasting joy by listening to the words of an archbishop. We can, I believe, find it if we let the cross speak to us and mould us and convince us that, with Jesus Christ as Lord, neither life nor death can ever defeat us.

Blasphemy or Creativity

□□□□

A CERTAIN BISHOP'S wife was taken to a ballet at the Kennedy Centre in Washington.[1] The performance nauseated her: she felt that both music and dance were offensive, and meaningless. Had she not been the guest of her companion she would have walked out half way through.

Afterwards, unable to contain herself, she asked, 'What was the point of all that?' 'Why,' said her companion, 'didn't it just cry aloud with the message of new birth and new love requiring the pre-condition of a death?' No, it had not cried aloud to the bishop's wife with any such thing; but to her companion it had stated solidly and evocatively the truth on which the Christian religion has been nourished for twenty centuries.

I believe that the whole issue of censorship of the arts is bedevilled by confusion of idiom with message. And it is extremely difficult for some people to accept that an idiom which is repulsive to them may be the most effective medium for conveying a vital insight to others. Put it the other way round. I suppose that 90 per cent of that Washington audience would have avoided a traditional Christian presentation of its central truth like the plague, as one avoids (if one can) anything that bores one silly. As it was, the ballet expressed an old and perennially valid idea in a contemporary metaphor which was enlightening to at least some of that 90 per cent.

What seems to me a bad thing is when a creative artist uses an excess of idiom intended to shock with a minimum of, or even an absence of, interior truth as he or she sees it.

Blasphemy, as opposed to sheer pornography, often lands on my desk, or, rather, letters arrive asking me to condemn what has appeared blasphemous in print or on television. And I am aware of the hurt that really hurts

[1] An article in *National Student*, March 1981

when the Person habitually worshipped in the beauty of holiness is profaned. But I repeat: an idiom that repels may still carry a writer's or an artist's honest search for, and affirmation of, a Christian truth. As a mild example of this, I remember the public shock when the artist Stanley Spencer portrayed Christ as the common man in the high-street. That was forty years ago. Now, in the 1980s, the high-street Christ has a perfectly respectable significance.

The justification of the Blasphemy Law is that the state shows its power to produce a context favourable to Christian belief, and that the mass of citizens are more disposed to respect that belief as plausible if the debasement of its chief symbols and concepts is discouraged by society. That is a reasonable position, given the reality of the claim that ours is a Christian society, as evidenced in the 1944 Education Act.

However, there are three reasons why I am usually unwilling to take the lead in condemning what appears blasphemous. The first is this: though I myself may not have discerned the intention of truth behind the repellent image, I know that other people may have got the message and found it valuable.

The second reason is a pragmatic one. For a long time the Church has somehow given the impression that it forbids, that it says no, that it is a confining influence rather than a creative one. Personal discipline must recognize the necessity of sometimes saying no: but I should like the public face of the institution to be seen as positive not negative, as creative not inhibiting. And there is something other than mere pragmatism in my belief that the Church itself should not be over-defensive. Remember that it was at its strongest when Jesus hung on the cross and they wagged their heads at him.

So the third reason to me carries the most weight. Traditional Christians in this country have *carte blanche* to portray Christ as they perceive him. In art, as in life, it is wide open to us to convey the appeal of holiness and beauty which we ourselves have experienced. If blasphemous material defaces the truth as we have seen it, there is nothing in the world to stop us from re-presenting the truth.

I think we should not complain. More constructively, we should use our *carte blanche* with a creativeness that compels attention. We really have everything on our side. And if with everything on our side we still feel threatened, the weakness must lie in ourselves. Could that weakness be a fatal laziness of the imagination?

Resurrection and Belief

🔲🔲🔲🔲

AN ARCHBISHOP IN England today is seldom personally attacked for the beliefs he holds.[1] No longer for him the sort of argument that can spring up in pub or club or student flat in which beliefs are fought for and jeered at in the cut and thrust of verbal debate. Like a general, an archbishop is removed from the arena of hand-to-hand fighting, and like a general he may sometimes regret this distancing.

The leaders of the early Church were not so insulated. If the credibility of their gospel was held in question they were told so in no uncertain terms and with contempt. At Corinth St Paul knew very well what made him a laughing stock: it was the preaching of the cross. Neither the Jew who looked for the sign of a triumphal Messiah nor the Greek who looked for disembodied wisdom could regard the humiliation of a crucified man other than as a stumbling-block and a foolishness.

I have an impression that the sticking point of our own times is a different one. A God made vulnerable to suffering is not today a barrier to belief: if there is a God, he must be one with whom humanity's pain and loneliness can identify. If the man in the street or on the board of management or at the high table laid aside his courtesy to me and allowed himself to jeer, I think it would not be at my acceptance of the events of Good Friday. More probably it would be at my credulity in accepting the events of Easter. He would say that he could not swallow the resurrection, and he might add that he doubted whether I could really swallow it either.

If I read the unspoken jeers rightly, the condemnation is a terrible one. For it means that what should be to our faith its very seal and patent of credibility has become the focus

[1] A meditation in the *Church Times*, April 1981

of incredulity. The Church has gained, has burgeoned, has won, only when its company has been seen to be the company of Easter people, and the individual Christian has only truly commended his or her faith when he or she is incontrovertibly seen as an Easter person.

What have we done, I wonder, to allow our Easterness to become blurred? Have we found that other aspects of our faith are more easily applied to the society in which we live, and in applying these seemingly more relevant aspects have we allowed the resurrection to become an optional extra? As we approach the morning when our churches will proclaim with a sort of new-washed gladness that Christ is risen, we do well to ask how authentic this gladness is to us; and if we ourselves are unable to respond to it we may ask why it is that we are missing out.

I believe that the Easter morning joy is likely to remain a hit-or-miss affair unless there is far more to it than the experience of one morning out of 365. Easter is not one aspect of our faith, an isolated event to be annually celebrated when the time comes round: unless the resurrection pervades and dominates our continuous stream of consciousness we shall indeed miss out, not only on Easter morning but throughout the whole fabric of our attempts at Christian life. Perhaps in an age such as ours, in which intellectual analysis tends always to dissect and existence itself seems to have lost its wholeness, we are particularly prone to fragmentation. But Easter does not speak of existence, it speaks of life: and life implies a single force, a unified power – a mainspring. If the risenness of Christ is not our mainspring, our faith can only at best jab here and there into different areas of fragmented existence, and our hope will be a fitful one. Without the resurrection our picture is chiaroscuro: if its light pervades and suffuses, we know what C. S. Lewis meant when he wrote: 'I believe in Christianity as I believe the sun has risen, not only because I see it but because by it I see everything else.'

This is all very well, we may say – who would not want to dance with the sun on Easter morning and on every morning of his life? – but unless the heart and mind are called to the dance the limbs can only go through the motions, and pretty leadenly at that. It is one thing to desire belief: it is another thing to be possessed of it. As the days progress towards Easter Sunday we may also ponder on the elusiveness of belief, its granting or its withholding.

I think that if we look for evidence of Easter we may see it more often than we recognize. Wherever, against all odds, the generous impulse overcomes the curmudgeonly instinct; where love conquers the grudge; where the go-getter becomes the giver; and wherever, after these small deaths, laughter and peace enhance the moment, there we may see small dazzling offshoots of the resurrection. For very often such behaviour does seem entirely against the odds and contrary to what we had expected. Newness of life is no less an astonishment than it is a delight.

We know that these surprises are given to us by non-Christians as well as by Christians. This does not lessen our thankfulness, but if our minds tease us for an explanation I believe it lies in the uncomprehended magnitude of God's mighty act in raising Jesus from the dead. It was a once-and-only act as far as history is concerned, but once enacted its power is limitless, not to be tied to our puny notions or expectancy. Let us regard the resurrection's continuous lavish overflow with wonder, but let us not wonder *at* it.

Does this then lessen the urgency for Christian commitment and belief? If a man or a woman can achieve selflessness for love's sake without commitment to creed and rule, does creed and rule matter very much? I think that a conscious relationship with the Lord of Life, and the feeding of this relationship in the Sacrament, should be our hearty desire for innumerable reasons: and here I suggest two out of many.

Relationship with the living Christ is to know that we cannot avoid those dark rooms of experience through which he has gone before: it is to discover in him that Easter morning comes only after Maundy evening and Good Friday. But in the conscious relationship we may also find that his resurrection power can, as it were, be harnessed and maximized. We ask, he gives: and in those who are closest to him we often notice that what might be an occasional possibility of achievement becomes a continuous certainty. 'As by your special grace going before us you put into our hearts good desires, so by your continued help we may bring the same to good effect.' I have heard that Easter Collect regretted, as bringing us down with too much of a bump from exaltation to a kind of mundane everydayness. But the words remind us that no longer need there be the slip between cup and lip, between the intention and the realization. The resurrection is not the memory of a story to be imitated as best we can, but an assurance of power conveyable to us by the available Presence. We ask; he of his risen power gives, and to know him whom we ask not only concentrates our asking but gives us a confident trust that we shall receive.

My second reason is brought to mind by the Easter alleluias. I believe that in this age, when mystery and transcendence are suspect, there still remains in the human make-up a profound need to worship. Granted the need, it would be mere contrivance to fix on Christ for the purpose of fulfilling that need. We must look at it the other way round, and call, if not on our own experience, on the observed experience of countless witnesses. It was from a context of doubt that the restored relationship of person to Person at once intensified into the words of worship, 'My Lord and my God'; and since the first recorded Easter meetings, the centuries have been spanned by a great host of witnesses, of those who have lived and died and lived again in a knowledge to which worship is always the first spontaneous reaction. It is not that the instinct to worship has at last contrived a focus but that the relationship once entered can be expressed in nothing else.

We have no power of ourselves – or, it seems, not quite enough power – to help ourselves, not even to belief. Belief remains a gift. We have perhaps just enough power to pray that God will fetch us to belief, or that he will fortify the belief we already hold. 'Let him Easter in us, be a dayspring to the dimness of us.' We ask; he alone and in his good time will give.

Easter Reality

🔲🔲🔲🔲

IT IS NOTORIOUSLY hard in art to portray the resurrection. There is an abundance of memorable representations of the cross and the Good Friday story, but far fewer images to help us with our celebrations.[1] There is one notable exception, however, which I wish were wider known. It is to be found in the church of Our Saviour in the Fields, an ancient Christian church in Istanbul. Amid some glorious Byzantine mosaics, there is a fresco of an incredibly vigorous and energetic Christ, pulling the parents of the human race, Adam and Eve, out of their tombs.

Sometimes, however, in recent Christian history, the resurrection story has been drained of the sap and reality very evident in that ancient fresco. The whole Easter story, from Good Friday to Easter Day, has been treated primarily as theatre, a symbolic presentation of the depth of God's love for suffering humanity. This is obviously part of the truth, but it is not enough. It waters down the scandal of the Christian faith and suggests that nothing really happened on that hilltop or in that tomb which changes anything. It is a superb story, which has engaged the passions of the devout through the ages who have undergone the kind of catharsis, the purging of emotion, which comes after watching a great tragedy. But it is not sufficient to say that Easter only works on human sensibilities, or that it can be said to involve simply the readjustment of human feelings. It was, and is, an act of God which changed the world.

So much of our religion now has lost the awesome sense and vision of God on the march, God acting. Instead, much religion has come to consist of putting on dramatic presentations and spectacles as teaching aids devised by religious professionals to explain to the rest of us about the

[1] Sermon in Canterbury Cathedral, Easter Sunday, 1982

nature of human community and the relationships and attitudes which can be derived from Christian doctrine. There is, of course, this element in all worship but I must confess that I was deeply shocked the other day when a priest said to me that he had given up daily Matins in his church 'because nobody came'. Worship should not just be a teaching aid. It binds heaven and earth together. We open the doors and windows of our spirit and prepare the house for the Lord to come in and dwell within us.

The emaciated understanding of worship is a reflection of a diluted Easter faith: Easter is not just theatre, or a demonstration. This way of looking at the events diminishes the reality, both of the suffering of Good Friday and of the victory of today. There was real suffering and degradation involved in the cross. Christ was crucified, not between two candlesticks on an altar, but between two thieves outside the city wall. Real suffering is inescapable if we are on the Christian way. If we have never recoiled from Good Friday then it is likely that we have never understood what happened and what is necessary and are not prepared for today.

The only thing at the first Easter which transformed the disillusioned friends and disciples of Jesus into a world-converting power was the reality of the resurrection. Here is no mere dramatic symbol of an eternal pattern of death and rebirth which can be discerned in nature. The Christian community was formed in the beginning by those who believed that God had acted to open the door through which man could pass to share in the divine life which not even death and time can quench. We believe that the world was charged with new possibilities at the first Easter. We celebrate today a turning-point in history.

But, the sceptic will say, nothing much in fact has changed in the last 2000 years to justify this assertion. Christians dispute that, and I should like to illustrate our faith by referring to two recent signs I have seen of resurrection power loose in the world.

Within the last week, I have been privileged to visit the oldest hospice for the dying in this country – St Joseph's, in Hackney. I met there a most remarkable lady, full of the confidence and faith that there *is* a door through which the followers of Christ can pass to be even closer to God and share in his divine life. She was an artist and a potter and I was moved almost to tears when she offered to give me her last work. She has now died and her last piece of pottery has arrived, containing a last testament of her faith, a broken eggshell. It is one of the most precious gifts I have ever received, a powerful expression of the resurrection faith that she has broken out of the shell, left behind her limitations and infirmities as she journeys into a fuller life in the sight of God.

The other sign is not so personal. There is hardly a country that has suffered more than Poland. It was reduced to rubble in the Second World War, but its ancient Christian Church has remained firm in its Easter convictions. The resurrection faith has rebuilt the rubble into a temple of spiritual power and energy which nothing in all creation can destroy. The political story of Poland still has many twists and checks ahead of it, but Christians believe that in the end nothing in the world can quench the hope which was given to us at the resurrection. We pray once more for the Polish people this Easter, but, what is more, we rejoice with them in our common faith.

Of course, this resurrection faith is not forced on us. We can deny its reality and stay immobilized by present problems and difficulties which seem too large for any human power to resolve. We can refuse to celebrate and can assert that we are alone, with God at best a convenient philosophical abstraction.

But what if we are not alone? What if life is not a challenge to cope on our own, but a challenge to co-operate with God? We hold out empty hands and they are grasped, as the hands of our first parents, Adam and Eve, were grasped by the virile Christ in the painting which has so haunted me throughout my ministry. We believe that this is the truth and that a Christian body, full of the spirit which flows in through Easter convictions, can do the impossible: bring new life out of the rubble left by human selfishness and aggression.

Christ is arisen. Alleluia! He is risen, not in the imagination alone, but in deed.

Suffering and Resurrection

⌑⌑⌑⌑

'FEAR NOT; I am the first and the last: I am he that liveth, and was dead; and, behold, I am alive for evermore, Amen; and have the keys of hell and of death.'

Encouragement was necessary. The first disciples experienced shock, astonishment and fear when they discovered the empty tomb and when they were confronted with the reality of the resurrection.

Since then, there have been nearly 2000 years of Christian history and, particularly in times of calm and relative security, the shock and reality of the resurrection is elaborated and explained and smoothed down. Sometimes, resurrection is understood just as a picture of some of the natural processes with which we are all familiar.

Some preachers on Easter Day talk of springtime – new life in nature – or the patient's experience of recovery from the depths when health returns or how, after a long struggle in a marriage, a new relationship blossoms.

In one moving meditation on the resurrection, there is this passage:

> We know it when doing a piece of work. We reach a point of utter frustration where the whole thing seems to be beyond us and we long to abandon it. But, if we don't abandon it, then almost at the very moment when we acknowledge our inability to go on, the whole thing buds and blossoms in our hands and we see a dozen ways in which to proceed.
>
> We know death and resurrection in our closest loves. In marriage perhaps in particular, we know what it is to struggle on when there are no rewarding emotions. And after, there comes a point where the relationship flowers gloriously beyond our imagination or expectation . . . and it is impossible afterwards to escape the knowledge that joy and happiness sprang out of the darkness of the pain.

¹ Sermon in Canterbury Cathedral, Easter Day, 1983

Certainly there are experiences of resurrection in all our lives and you don't have to be a Christian to experience them. The resurrection of Jesus Christ, however, is not just a way of drawing attention to some of the recurrent patterns of human experience. It is a unique event which brings hope of a kind that cannot be extracted from the world of natural processes.

I remind you of this because one of the great difficulties which people find in our time when they consider the claims of belief is the way in which the vocabulary of Christianity has been gradually diluted into a mere series of ethical truisms and made to mean what it never meant before. The end of this process is that the message becomes so thin and anaemic that there is really no reason, no impetus, to believe in something that has practically no content.

When the resurrection is simply a spiritual event within the hearts of disciples, and when everything is translated into non-historical terms, then the gospel becomes one more fairy-tale. If you treat the gospel in this way, then it is arguable that there are more entertaining fairy-tales presented with even greater literary artifice.

The gospel which brought the Christian Church into being is proclaiming something which is beyond us and which has the effect of widening our vision at times beyond the bearable. The trouble is that when you add too much water to a glass of wine, it gradually becomes water tainted with wine. It gives you none of the kick which a glass of wine can give.

If God becomes just one of our ideas, imprisoned in the world of cause and effect, and resurrection just an allegory of certain recurrent patterns in human experience, then hope for the human enterprise is short indeed.

Men are always being tempted to live out the lie that they are gods. They try to live as if they are at the centre of the universe; like medieval astronomers, they are tempted to believe that the sun revolves around them. God, if he has a place at all, is a Sunday secret for those people who have a taste for religion as a hobby. Again and again, this arrogance is revealed for what it is and seen to have very bitter consequences.

We are near the end of an historical period in the West in

which there has been a particularly vigorous attempt to assert that the sun should orbit around us. For the last 300 years, man has been seeking, through the exercise of his God-given intellect, to manage and control his environment. We now dominate our planet in a way that no previous generation has done. In human organization, we have the capacity to guarantee a reasonable standard of living for all the people in the world. There is doubt, however, about whether we have the will and spiritual energy to do so. But our capacities also extend to a power to regulate the lives of individual human beings as never before. Tragically, man's progress towards god-like management of his fellows and of nature itself has, in our own day, culminated in the unleashing of seemingly unmanageable forces. Nuclear weapons and the horrifying prospect of nuclear warfare are, of course, the most eloquent symbol of this tragic development, but the tragedy can also be seen in the capacity of totalitarian states to subject their subjects to previously undreamed-of manipulation and social engineering which no moral wisdom can possibly control or justify.

If God were trapped in the world of cause and effect, as just another of our ideas of ourselves as god-like, then there would be little hope indeed.

But: 'Fear not,' said Jesus, 'I am the first and the last.' God stands before history and he is the meaning of history. Christ is not to be imprisoned. He has the keys even of death and of hell.

This truth is most obvious and invisible in places and in times when man's effort to become god-like has been exposed as a tragic distortion of the real order of things. The reality of the resurrection and the hope it brings was experienced by the author of the Book of Revelation who spoke to us in the First Lesson. He belonged to a community that was facing the persecution of the Roman state which had pretended to god-like power to the extent even of deifying its emperors. John the Divine was in exile in the island of Patmos. He had tasted the 'tribulation' and was in prison 'for the Word of God and for the testimony of Jesus Christ'. It was then in some Roman Gulag that John was encouraged and sustained by the risen Christ and used by him as his spokesman.

It is not necessary, however, to go back many centuries to find places where the reality of the resurrection has blazed up in the darkness created by the lie that man is a god with no dependence upon the will and word of the Creator. Two places which experience that resurrection faith now are South Africa and the Soviet Union.

My brother Anglican Bishop in South Africa, Desmond Tutu, once said to me that he would find it hard to be a Christian in England where everything was so complicated and ill defined. He believed that it was easier to be a Christian in South Africa. Those are the words of a very courageous man and, as you will probably know, a man who is currently facing the test. A delegation drawn from various parts of the Anglican Communion has been sent by me to South Africa to demonstrate our solidarity with Bishop Tutu. They have just returned with an encouraging report of the strengths of the Easter faith despite all difficulties.

But perhaps the most vivid experience of the resurrection reality known to me is in the Soviet Union. Michael Bourdeaux has just written an important book called *Risen Indeed: Lessons in Faith from the USSR*. I would advise everybody to read it. No plausible stories can disguise the fact that the Church in the Soviet Union in recent times has experienced very great suffering. Solzhenitsyn, in his Nobel Prize lecture, refers in his oblique way to 'one place where not so long ago there were persecutions no less severe than those of ancient Rome, in which hundreds of thousands of Christians gave their lives in silence because of their faith in God'. In these circumstances, I share with Michael Bourdeaux the perception that Russian Christians do not debate the resurrection. They have experienced its reality in their own lives. 'They have not preserved the faith in hostile surroundings, it has preserved them.'

Christians, like the first disciples, like St John the Divine on the island of Patmos, like Bishop Desmond Tutu, like many Christians in the Soviet Union, know of a God who is not just an idea in the human mind but a God who cares, a God who acts and a God who saves. Their joy at the resurrection event is profound and not genteel. They can teach us that joy and many other things.

I end with one of the lessons in faith from the USSR: Michael Bourdeaux was standing in a church in total darkness, on Easter Eve:

> A hammering and creaking from the back indicated a great door opening. 'Whom seek ye?' 'The body of Jesus.' 'Why seek ye the living among the dead? He is not here, he is risen.' For the first time, the great crowd broke its silence. A murmur as though they could not believe the truth they were affirming. 'He is risen indeed' was their antiphon. But now too there was light. Someone at the back had lit the first Paschal candle . . . swiftly the flame passed from hand to hand . . . each candle lit up a face behind it. That face bore the deep lines of sorrow, of personal tragedy. Yet, as it was illuminated, the suffering turned to joy, to the certain knowledge of the reality of the risen Lord.

We have been given a faith which is strong enough for the darkest shadows in life. I pray that familiarity may not blunt the wonder of an astonishing message which we celebrate together in Canterbury today.

The Queen Mother

🔲🔲🔲🔲

I HAPPENED TO be present recently when the Queen Mother[1] was paying a visit to Kent. She said she was looking forward to further visits and to getting to know the area better, particularly now that she had been appointed Warden of the Cinque Ports. At a time of life when many people have already been retired for twenty years, the Queen Mother continues to display an astonishing taste for new experiences and new friendships, so much so that it would probably be more accurate to say that we are met to celebrate and give thanks for the Queen Mother's *first* eighty years.

On the same occasion, I heard a woman in the crowd make a remark which stuck in my mind and has given me my theme: 'It's a lovely dress, of course, but I just can't take my eyes off her *face*. She looks so cheerful.' Queen Elizabeth's face is known and loved throughout the world and has been endlessly reproduced in every medium from oil painting to postage stamp. In a particularly graceful birthday tribute, the National Portrait Gallery has organized an exhibition of portraits of the Queen Mother which is well worth a visit and which illustrates vividly one of the main functions of royalty.

Royalty puts a *human face* on the operations of government and provides images with which the people of a nation can identify and which they can love. The Queen Mother has over the years helped us to feel that being a citizen of this country is not just being an entry on the central computer, or being an income tax code number, but it is being a member of *a family* where common interests and kinships exist beneath and beyond all our divisions and conflicts. It is very difficult to fall in love with committees

---

[1] Sermon preached to celebrate the eightieth birthday of Queen Elizabeth, the Queen Mother, St Paul's Cathedral, 15 July 1980

or policies, but the Queen Mother has shown a human face which has called out the loyalty and the sense of belonging without which a nation loses its heart and disintegrates.

It is a sobering thought that although we begin life with a certain natural endowment – a bone structure, skin colour, a certain kind of flesh tissue – as life goes on *we* play a larger and larger part in making our own faces. Our faces reflect the influence under which we have been living: our sufferings and the attitude to life we have taken up. The Queen Mother has been no stranger to suffering of a kind that comes to most of us, notably bereavement, but she has accepted what has befallen her and been able to turn it into uncondescending and lively sympathy for the misfortunes of others. I shall always remember her famous remark after the bombing of Buckingham Palace during the Second World War: 'I'm glad we have been bombed, it makes me feel we can look the East End in the face.' That woman in the crowd I mentioned when I began saw a face which had its share of the dignity that comes from suffering, but one which was *also* full of life, affection and cheerfulness and a zest for new things and people.

Cynics and pessimists have been in plentiful supply in recent decades, and sometimes the negativity they express has been confused with sophistication. Hardly any of the institutions of our national life have escaped satire or mockery. The monarchy and the royal family have not been exempt from this kind of criticism, but the Queen Mother has continued to speak and stand for abiding virtues and to express her confidence in things that are pure, things that are lovely, things that are of good report.

The faith and the hope which are evident in her way of doing her work can *appear* simple and naive, like the text from Julian of Norwich which began this service: 'All shall be well and all shall be well, and all manner of things shall be well.' It may be simple but it is not naive, as you will see if you consider the contrast between the satirist indulging in repeats and revivals, and the Queen Mother appearing as fresh and forward-looking as ever. By reflecting the great simplicities of faith and goodness, and never simply following the trend, she has occupied the centre of the stage since 1923 without suffering the fate which so frequently befalls the fashionable personality who is played out after ten years or so in public life.

Faith, hope and love which are deep and nourishing are God-given, they come in full measure to those who are turned in the direction of God, *and it shows*. Without being insensitive to suffering, we need encouraging examples that human life is *intended* to be full of delight and celebration: Creator and creature rejoicing over one another in a bond of love. How can we be thankful enough for the Queen Mother's love of life and people in all its rich variety: the dogs and the horses, the flowers, the gardens, the fishing, the pictures and the music? Nothing narrow or second-rate, but unselfconscious artistry in her care for details, her unique capacity to relate to all ages and races – student, scholar, housewife or statesman – and an amazing memory for faces. As much at home in the countryside as in palaces, and ever cherishing a lifelong love affair with Scotland. A human face of deep but unparaded faith, equally able to worship in a splendid cathedral like this, with all its memories, or in a simple Presbyterian chapel over the Border.

The Queen Mother reminds us of a basic religious truth. If you want to know the inmost nature of God you must not look so much to rules, commandments and principles, important as they are; instead you must look at the faces of those who love God and whose lives have been nourished by his life, supremely, of course, as St Paul writes: 'The light of the knowledge of the glory of God shining in the face of Jesus Christ.' All of us fall short, and the Queen Mother would be the first to want me to say that. Yet the Queen Mother has reflected *something* of that love which comes from those who try to live facing God. What we have seen in one greatly loved and universally admired lady is a love which has been given through her to us, and returned to her by us, and then given again by her, over and over again. Queen Elizabeth I said: 'Though God has raised me high, yet this I count the glory of my crown, that I have reigned with your loves.' I know that is as true today of the Queen Mother, as of us.

I am conscious that I have not said all that some of you would have wished me to say. But I take heart from some words which Queen Elizabeth herself wrote in a foreword to a certain anthology. She wrote there of 'what in our hearts we believe, but find so hard to say'. And it was there she added: 'We can at one and the same time be truly contemporary men and women *and* have our thoughts and lives rooted in truths that do not change.'

The Royal Wedding

🔲🔲🔲🔲

HERE IS THE stuff of which fairy-tales are made: the Prince and Princess on their wedding day.[1] But fairy-tales usually end at this point with the simple phrase, 'They lived happily ever after'. This may be because fairy-stories regard marriage as an anti-climax after the romance of courtship. This is not the Christian view. Our faith sees the wedding day not as the place of arrival but the place where the adventure really begins.

There is an ancient Christian tradition that *every* bride and groom on their wedding day are regarded as a royal couple. To this day in the marriage ceremonies of the Eastern Orthodox Church crowns are held over the man and the woman to express the conviction that as husband and wife they are kings and queens of creation. As it says of humankind in the Bible, 'Thou crownedst him with glory and honour, and didst set him over the work of thy hands.'

On a wedding day it is made clear that God does not intend us to be puppets but chooses to work through us, and especially through our marriages, to create the future of this world. Marriage is first of all a new creation for the partners themselves. As husband and wife live out their vows, loving and cherishing one another, sharing life's splendours and miseries, achievements and setbacks, they will be transformed in the process. A good marriage is a life, as the poet Edwin Muir says:

> Where each asks from each
> What each most wants to give;
> And each awakes in each
> What else would never be.

But any marriage which is turned in upon itself, in which the bride and groom simply gaze obsessively at one

---

[1] Address given at the marriage of the Prince of Wales and the Lady Diana Spencer, St Paul's Cathedral, 29 July 1981

another, goes sour after a time. A marriage which really works is one which works for others. Marriage has both a private face and a public importance. If we solved all our economic problems and failed to build loving families, it would profit us nothing, because the family is the place where the future is created good and full of love – or deformed.

Those who are married live happily ever after the wedding day if they persevere in the real adventure which is the royal task of creating each other and creating a more loving world. That is true of every man and woman undertaking marriage. It must be especially true of this marriage in which are placed so many hopes.

Much of the world is in the grip of hopelessness. Many people seem to have surrendered to fatalism about the so-called inevitabilities of life: cruelty, injustice, poverty, bigotry and war. Some have accepted a cynical view of marriage itself. But all couples on their wedding day are 'royal couples' and stand for the truth that we help to shape this world and are not just its victims. All of us are given the power to make the future more in God's image and to be 'kings and queens' of love.

This is our prayer for Charles and Diana. May the burdens we lay on them be matched by the love with which we support them in the years to come. However long they live, may they always know that when they pledged themselves to each other before the altar of God they were surrounded and supported not by mere spectators but by the sincere affection and active prayer of millions of friends.

The Language of Music

🮮🮮🮮🮮

SERMONS DIVIDE WHERE music unites. That was one of the
messages of my predecessor, Archbishop Tait, at the
meeting which founded the Royal College of Music, a
hundred years ago today.[1] It is true he undermined his
authority by admitting he was tone deaf. I cannot claim to be
a musicologist, but at least I do not labour under my
distinguished predecessor's difficulty and, being married to
a musician, I have a resident tutor.

Archbishop Tait was, of course, right: music in itself
unites diverse forces and themes. The process of com-
position binds together a variety of instruments in the
orchestra and brings harmony out of an interplay of
musical ideas, sub-plots and leitmotifs. Music also clearly
transcends cultural and linguistic divisions: you do not
need to know German to appreciate Beethoven. But I wish
to spend the time allotted to me in considering another
barrier which music can surmount.

The Royal College of Music was launched with words.
The meeting convened by the Prince of Wales at St James's
Palace in 1882 was a veritable *Gabfest*. One hundred years
later, we are celebrating the centenary with music and the
preacher has been warned to confine himself to a modest
ten minutes. I do so gladly and willingly, for a very
important reason. During the last one hundred years we
have been battered by words – newspapers, radio programmes, advertisements and election addresses – so we
are properly suspicious of rhetoric and the obfuscating
jargon of bureaucracies and official organizations. We are
constantly being challenged and called in words, but very
often we fail to be convinced by them.

Music, by contrast, does not evoke such weary cynicism.

---

[1] Lecture delivered at the Royal College of Music, at its centenary service,
28 February 1982

We are, in large numbers, receptive to music in a way in which we are not receptive to words. Music has become available, not just to an élite but, as the founders of the Royal College envisaged and worked for, music is now the property of vast numbers of people in our country. Through a standard of performance and virtuosity which must be without equal in our history, through the concert hall, the long-playing record and radio, music has become available to millions and, for them, it constitutes a door through a world soiled, defined and imprisoned by definitions, into those uplands described by Elgar and Vaughan Williams where even the sombre shades are somehow more intense and more elevating.

One hundred years ago, music occupied a lowlier place in our national life than it does now. Long past were the days of the seventeenth century, when music was still considered to be a key to understanding the universe and when there was still some lingering respect for music which had been a central and integral part of medieval education. The poet Dryden, in his 'Saint Cecelia Day Song' for 1687, represented the end of this ancient tradition:

> From harmony, from heavenly harmony,
> This universal frame began:
> From harmony to harmony
> Through all the compass of the notes it ran,
> The diapason closing full in Man.

This rather exalted language reminds us of music's particularly close relationship as a handmaid to religious sentiment but, by the eighteenth century, music had been somewhat degraded either to a rather undistinguished role in church or to the status of a mere amusement. By the eighteenth century, man might or might not have an ear for music, just as he might or might not have a leaning to piety. English music in this period became a rather dull echo of continental trends, or actually relied upon the importation of continental masters like Handel.

This pattern remained virtually unchanged until the later years of the nineteenth century. England did not share in the revolutionary ardours of the end of the eighteenth century which on the Continent produced a

seismic shift to the grand and romantic music associated
with Beethoven and his followers. We were rather a
musical backwater when Wesley's anthem, 'Blessed be the
God and Father', was first sung in Hereford Cathedral on
Easter Day, 1833. The only adult member of the choir
present was a single bass, the Dean's butler. On another
occasion, at St Paul's, Handel's 'Hallelujah Chorus' was
chosen for the anthem, but during the service a message
was sent to Goss in the organ-loft that only one tenor and
one bass were present. 'Do your best,' he replied, 'and I will
do the rest with the organ.' No wonder that Mr Gladstone,
speaking at the meeting which inaugurated the Royal
College, said, when describing the state of church music, 'I
cannot use any epithet weaker than one that may perhaps
shock the meeting.'

One of the specific objects of the founding of the Royal
College of Music was the elevation in the standards of
church choirs, but I suspect that there was something
much deeper involved. Music was no longer an amusement,
or a *divertissement*; it was once again central to a culture
which needed to escape from the imprisonment of rationality
and definition and analysis. It is significant that many of
the great students of the Royal College have found it
difficult to affirm any Christian conviction in creed or
words, but in their music they have, it seems, been drawn
irresistibly not only to the texts of the liturgy but also, like
Vaughan Williams or Benjamin Britten, to an attempt to
express the mystery and wonder that lies on the margins of
the desert created by prose.

Music is for so many the door into the realm of the spirit;
their way over the boulders and obstacles deposited by a
century of linguistic criticism. Browning saw this when he
wrote a hundred years ago:

Sorrow is hard to bear, and doubt is slow to clear,
Each sufferer says his say, his scheme of the weal and woe:
But God has a few of us whom he whispers in the ear;
The rest may reason and welcome: 'tis we musicians know.

Windows onto God

🎀🎀🎀🎀

CANONS AND OTHERS who serve our cathedrals[1] now, need to combine the virtues of an oriental guru with the dynamism of an entrepreneur. Cathedrals now once more attract vast numbers of visitors as they did in the Middle Ages. Now, as then, it is difficult and pointless to make any sharp distinction between pilgrims and holidaymakers. They are drawn to a meeting place for many arts, for music, for painting and sculpture, but anyone who spends time talking to visitors in a place like this knows that they are not just coming to a concert hall or an art gallery.

In the contemporary search for meaning and vision, cathedrals are places where many puzzled or honestly curious people can come to look and listen without being sucked into the premature commitment almost inescapable in a small-scale community church. In this place you minister to the often inarticulate craving of our generation for order and vision. Here you welcome people who are often beyond the reach of the local church and the very stones can talk about God without a word being said. This is very important. There are so many words which come at us in a daily deluge from press and broadcasting that we have become resistant to them. Many words have indeed become threadbare and congregational tolerance for too many of them has become thin. When John Donne the poet was Dean of St Paul's he once preached for two hours in the open air outside the cathedral and when he showed signs of drawing to a conclusion, the congregation cried out: 'More, more!' I doubt whether nowadays even the most gifted preachers have such experiences often.

When we wish to express our experience of the sublimity of God, his glory and beauty, the most eloquent way is

---

[1] Sermon preached at the Final Thanksgiving Service of Wells 800, Wells Cathedral, 30 November 1982

often in stone, in music, in stained glass, in colour and movement. This is what you have been doing at Wells during the past eight months of your festival, certainly in the specifically religious works like Elgar's 'Dream of Gerontius', but also in the other parts of the musical programme and in the various exhibitions. Above all, the very stones of this beautiful Cathedral of St Andrew, its history and beauty, can stimulate the delight and wonder which tip over into prayer. In places like the Soviet Union where many restrictions are placed on the preaching of the gospel, the church buildings still speak in their beauty when even the bells have been silenced.

There was a fashion some years ago for bemoaning the costly inheritance the Church of England has received in its ancient places of worship. The critics lumped churches and cathedrals together under the heading 'plant' and resented the time and energy spent on their upkeep. 'Plant' suggests something entirely functional, but it should be clear to everyone that this cathedral does not merely exist to keep the rain off and to shelter large gatherings of people: it is an expression in stone of the delight which a man knows when he knows God and when he knows that God loves him and has a purpose for him which is nothing less than a share in his divine life.

In preaching a sermon, however, I am obviously affirming that there is a necessary partnership between words and the non-verbal windows onto God. Worship, the offices of Matins and Evensong and the celebration of Holy Communion, has gone on throughout the festival. Any church or cathedral is a place where God is named and where God calls. In the Lesson, for example, we heard the call to St Andrew which has resonated throughout 2000 years and which the Christian believer hears as a call to himself. When performed in the cathedral where God is named and where he calls, a piece of music can be given new depths as an expression of the harmony and beauty which belongs to the author and creator of all things. It can also be given a new edge as something which recalls us to our own state of disharmony and spoilt spiritual beauty. Music just by itself cannot do this. It can sometimes just evoke agreeable sensations. There were concentration camp commandants who enjoyed Mozart in the evenings after work. But in a cathedral where God is named, music can refer us to the depths of the design and open up new horizons.

You can see that I believe that the arts are a vital element in the Church's teaching about God. In an age of space travel and the uncovering of the seemingly unlimitless vastness of outer space, our concepts about God have been revealed as too small and our images too domesticated. The image of God as an old man with a white beard, in the sky, is a fact which still helps many people to draw closer to their heavenly Father. The difficulty arises when people reject that image and believe that they have rejected God. It is simply that their God is too small for the vastness and complexity that has been revealed. Music and the other arts in this situation can help to nourish our imaginations and help point us to a God whose power and wisdom is consummate with the immensity of space.

It is possible to prove or disprove the existence of God by philosophical argument. The Bible never attempts to come to God in this way. In the biblical view, there are signs of his presence, for those with the eyes to see them, all around us, and conviction grows and deepens as we struggle to see all our knowledge and experience, our wonder and our suffering in relation to him. Century after century and here in Wells for more than a millennium, men and women have discovered that God and human life belong together. They have discovered delight and a meaning for their sufferings in the conviction that God has created us for himself and our hearts find no rest until they rest in him. Without God, however much we are distracted by comfort or the feelings stimulated by an efficient dance band and the entertainment industry, we are really alone, treading the water in an ocean which is miles deep and where no land is to be seen. Without God we are condemned to a life which comes from a chemical accident and which rapidly passes into nothing.

If we embrace God, then we can discover a depth of meaning and wonder and a hope which the world cannot give. You can only really test the truth of a statement like that by tasting and seeing. We are often armour-plated against the experiment of tasting and seeing when the call is made to us in words. We have worked out our answers long ago, and being experimental takes energy and courage. People say with pride that they are sceptical, and often, when presented with a theological proposition about God, their scepticism expresses itself in the question, 'Suppose it isn't true?' But the true sceptic, and this is one of those simple spiritual truths which is so obvious that it is hardly ever seen, the true sceptic also spends time exploring the question, 'Suppose it is true?' Does the idea of God the Creator fit into the world of mingled wonder and pain that I know? Often it is easier to experiment in this direction while listening to Handel's 'Israel in Egypt' or while looking at a great religious picture, or reflecting on the 800 years of this church and the people who built it. All these things are windows onto heaven. They supply a language to express what lies beyond words.

So we have good cause to give thanks for this festival; for the times in the last eight months when God has disclosed more of his glory; we thank God for the sap and savour which comes to life with the conviction that when the last useful thing has been done in this world, when the last committee has sat and the last royal commission reported, there will still remain the love of God, the delight and wonder which gave birth to the universe. We pray that as a church we shall be more and more marked by the vision we have seen and so draw others to the joy of loving God as he has loved us. It was for that reason, for he is no utilitarian, that Christ the Son of God came into the world. 'Jesus said, "I am come that they might have life and that they might have it more abundantly."'